PERFECT RESUMES

&

SUCCESSFUL INTERVIEWS

RAY BIRKINSHA

PERFECT RESUMES & *SUCCESSFUL INTERVIEWS*
By Ray Birkinsha

Ray Birkinsha
MileStones Press LLC
ray@milestonespress.com

Copyright © 2013

All rights reserved. No part of this book may be reproduced or transmitted in any form or by any means, electronic or mechanical, including photocopying, recording or any information storage and retrieval system, without written permission from the author.

ISBN 978-0-9840960-1-5

First Edition
Printed in the United States of America

Contents

Finding a Job Is a Full-Time Job 1
Step By Step—From Resume to Offer 3
Job Hunting Skills 7
Your Perfect Job 9
Networking 11
Marketing Yourself 15
Where to Look 22
Boundaries 30
Be Confident 33
Burning Bridges 38
The Decision-Maker 40
Creating a Job—Rob's Story 43
Rejection 46
Your Image 50

Perfect Resumes

The Perfect Resume 55
Take Inventory 58
Adding Value 61
Big Company vs. Small Company 65
Format and First Impressions 70
The Model Resume 78
The Tailored Resume 85
The Online Resume 91
The Leap Frog Resume 93
The Over Qualified Resume 96
Resume Issues 98
The Cover Letter 105
References 107

SUCCESSFUL INTERVIEWS

INTERVIEWING STRATEGY 111
ANSWERING QUESTIONS 113
PREPARE, PREPARE, PREPARE 118
BE ORGANIZED 120
TELL STORIES 122
PRACTICE, PRACTICE, PRACTICE 128
THE SCREENING/TELEPHONE INTERVIEW 135
THE INTERVIEW 137
TOUGH QUESTIONS 141
ISSUES 148
INTERVIEW MISTAKES 149
FOLLOWING UP 151
PERFECT RESUMES & SUCCESSFUL INTERVIEWS 153

APPENDIX 1   YOUR TARGET—YOUR DREAM JOB 154
APPENDIX 2   YOUR PERSONAL INVENTORY 156
APPENDIX 3   PRACTICE INTERVIEW QUESTIONS 161

Forward

This book is about finding a job. It focuses on resumes and interviews, but it covers the whole process of marketing yourself to potential employers and being successful in your job search. Everything you do to prepare, improve yourself and plan is not only part of the job hunting process . . . it has a significant impact on your resume and your ability to sell yourself in interviews.

This is not a book with "get a job quick" tips. Finding a job today is a hard process But companies are hiring and most companies will hire someone who can help them be profitable or increase their chances of survival.

This is a book about the basics, and the basics are submitting resumes and getting interviewed.

I've heard that some experts think resumes are passé. There are professions where employers request videos or use social media to identify potential employees, but most employers won't move away from resumes and interviews any time soon. Employers like the compactness of a resume. They can sort through them quickly and most still rely on resumes to make their initial interviewing decisions, to prepare questions for interviews, and take notes on them so they can remember candidates.

You have to be aware of how employers use technology to handle resumes and screen candidates. Computer programs are increasingly used to reduce good resumes to their basic information and to search for key words—although I think that how well a resume is prepared should be important to an employer. You need to know which fonts to use and how to format a resume so it'll look good and so software programs can read it and sort the data correctly.

Some experts opine on format, word choice, and current trends and fashions in preparing resumes. I was listening to an expert the other day who pronounced that it was no longer fashionable to use a summary on a resume. The problem with these opinions is that many employers don't know what's fashionable! Most decision-makers have been around for a while. They know what they expect when they solicit resumes and if you send a "fashionable" resume it may not help you get an interview.

Which brings me to an important question—why did I write this book? My expertise started almost twenty years ago when I sat in a corporate lunchroom and was told that everyone in my company was being let go! We were being asked to reapply for our jobs; with new titles and lower pay. The idea was to get rid of non-performing employees and save money on the rest of us. I was asked to put together a program about resumes and interviews for those about to move on. I did the program, took the severance and found a better job!

For the last twenty years I've been writing, mentoring, hiring, interviewing and speaking about these topics. I'm a lawyer by training, an executive by experience and an expert on getting hired by choice.

One important point that I'll repeat throughout this book; no resume and no interview strategy will succeed all the time. People will review your resume and make a quick and often wrong judgment about your qualifications. Sometimes you win and sometimes you lose. The successful resume gets you an interview. The successful interview puts you in contention. If you send out enough resumes and get enough interviews eventually you'll get an offer—and that's the objective of all this hard work.

You can do it. You can be successful if you'll apply basic principles and give it all you've got. You only fail when you give up. So don't give up.

FINDING A JOB IS A FULL-TIME JOB

For most of us, job-hunting is more of a hobby that's done when the weather, stars and our mood are all in alignment. And heaven forbid that it should actually require hard work or uncomfortable tasks. If you're unemployed or looking for better employment, you have to approach job-hunting like a real job; where the objective is to find yourself a job.

Think of it as hiring yourself; you are now the management and entire workforce for YOU—a company with the sole mission of finding your dream job.

Here's your new job description:

> Wanted: Enthusiastic sales and marketing professional willing to work 20-80 hours a week for NO pay to make one sale. Flexible hours, great educational benefits. Writing and interviewing skills a plus. Must be able to think outside self-perceptions and able to handle lots of rejection.

The good news is that you're uniquely qualified for this job and no one else wants the job of finding you a job for no pay!

Your full-time focus is to find your next job. It has to be more than a part-time, casual activity; unless you have a job and then finding another one is a part-time job. You need to be the most demanding manager you've ever had. And when you have a heart to heart with yourself, you need to ask yourself if your actions are helping you get where you want to be? Are you moving yourself closer to a new career or not?

As with any job, you're not going to spend forty hours a week doing one thing, like searching job postings. You're the management and sales force of your operation, so there are many administrative and product improvement activities you have to do. In fact, it's not just a job—it's a business. Your business. You're self-employed and everything that gets done, gets done by you!

So what are your new responsibilities? You understand that you need to submit resumes, applications and go through interviews. But what else do you do to be successful?

Job Duties of the CEO of YOU, Inc.

Preparation	*Job Hunting*	*Product Development*
Marketing materials	Finding Prospects	Evaluation
Product research	Calls	Networking
Prospect research	Interviews	Education
Practice	Make one sale . . .	Skill development

Job-finding responsibilities fall into three broad categories.

The first is preparation, which includes research, resume writing, education, role-playing—whatever you can do to be more competitive in your search and in interviews.

The second category consists of actual job-hunting—responding to job posts, interviewing, going door-to-door if you have to.

The third category is product improvement—the time you spend making yourself more valuable to potential employers: taking classes, finishing a professional designation or studying professional materials.

When you have a strategy and stick to it, these activities will easily take the time and effort of a full-time job . . . and then some. It's not enough to check the new job posts on a couple of websites and send out a couple of resumes. Finding a job requires selling your ability to add value, solve problems and overcome obstacles—which are the skills you need to be successful in finding a job!

STEP BY STEP—FROM RESUME TO OFFER

For employers, getting to the real candidates is a process of elimination. Employers use screening techniques to get the applicant pool down to a workable number. One of HR's jobs is to be an obstacle, part of the screening process. From the initial job description, which eliminates as many people as possible to the multiple reviews and interviews, the process is designed to get to a small number of final candidates. To get through these obstacles and reach the decision-makers you need to understand the process.

Procedures differ for various employers and positions. In some cases you get to the decision-maker quickly, but most managers create and use barriers in large part because they don't want to spend all of their time reviewing resumes or interviewing candidates.

The Purpose of a Resume Is to Get an Interview

This is a critical concept to understand: *your resume won't get you a job*. Getting a job offer comes after an employer makes you jump through hoops to get to know who you are. The purpose of your resume is to get you to those hoops—starting with the first interview.

To do that, your resume needs to quickly and easily demonstrate that you:

- ✓ Meet the job requirements.
- ✓ Will add value to the organization.
- ✓ Don't have any flaws that can be inferred from your resume.

It's a bonus if you are a clear standout with prestigious degrees and awards. But an amazing resume won't get you a job, just an interview.

Interview to Get the Next Interview

Your goal at each step is to get to the next step. If you try to shorten the process by being overly aggressive or by assuming you have the job from the first phone interview, you won't make the cut because you're working from the wrong assumptions and not keeping your eye on the target. Let me repeat: your goal is to get to the next step in the process.

When you get a phone call that an employer wants to interview you, find out how their process works: how many rounds are there and who will you be talking to in each round? Larger companies often use HR to conduct the first interviews, usually over the telephone. Your first interview with an HR representative is a screening process. HR will contact a large pool of acceptable resumes then cut the field down. You want to speak well, confirm the information in your resume and not make big mistakes.

As you get into the subsequent rounds of interviews, each round becomes more important because the "points" earned during each interview add up, so every round counts.

The section on Successful Interviews will help you prepare to interview well. Don't lose sight of your goal, which is to get through all of the hoops and make it to the finish line—an accepted job offer.

Follow up after Every Interview

The reason for sending a follow-up is to keep you in the mind of the interviewer and to provide evidence of your professionalism. Get the names, titles and contact information for every person you talk to. Know the name of the person who sets up appointments and who you should contact if something comes up (don't let anything come up). After an interview, follow up with a written thank you. You can send material or information that was discussed in the interview, like letters of reference, articles, books or work product you talked about. Make sure your communication is relevant, emphasizes your themes and message and is professional.

The Final Interview Is Not a Job Offer

When you're one of the last candidates for a position you get excited. But don't start dreaming about all that money yet, because you still need to get to the last stage in the hiring process—the offer. Don't assume you have the job. Don't let your guard down, get casual or arrogant. Being a finalist is a good thing, but in the job hunting game only the winner gets a prize and until you accept a job offer, there's still a sale to be made.

Know who you're meeting for the final interview. This is the round where the decision-maker's boss may get involved, so be prepared. Don't start negotiating salary before you have the offer, don't talk about redecorating the office (I've had it happen!) and don't get too casual . . . blowing a good opportunity because of an inappropriate comment or joke.

The Offer

Don't start negotiating before you have an offer, and don't lose the offer by overestimating your ability to change it.

Second and third place applicants don't usually get a call until all of the details are worked out with the winner. If an employer is delaying after the final interviews, it may mean that the decision-makers went on vacation, but it can mean you're close—and still in the running—if the winner blows it.

By the time you get to the final interview, you should know what the position is, where the job is located and have a pretty good idea of the employer's salary range. The issue to be negotiated is where your salary falls in that range—usually not *what* the range is. If salary or wage is an issue, it should come up before the offer. Employers get mad when you demand far above their anticipated pay, especially if they've been clear from the beginning.

What if they told you a range and approach you with an offer that's well below it? That's a problem that's more common in a tight job market. Ask for clarification about the sudden change. If I thought I had other options or there were other problems with the offer, I'd probably decline it. But if I need the job, I might take it. There's less loyalty when an employment relationship starts this way—I'd probably keep looking for my dream job.

Don't Stop Looking

This isn't so much about the interview process as keeping your head in the game. We all tend to let up a little when we reach the final rounds of an interview process. If the job entails a move, I start looking at houses. And sometimes we put our job search on hold. Don't do it. Until you accept an offer you're still a self-employed job hunter. Keep sending out resumes, contacting, networking and interviewing. This prevents you from losing time and opportunities if you don't get an offer. And it lessens the inevitable impact of being so close and not getting an offer. Stay in control, stay engaged and deal with offers *when* they come, not before.

Getting through all of these hoops is a process. It's also a numbers game. It takes a certain number of resumes to get an interview, a certain amount of initial interviews will result in making it to the final round, and it may require a number of times in the finals to win the prize. Be persistent. Don't lose sight of what you're trying to accomplish at each stage. Be patient, take each step in the process and you'll get an offer.

Job Hunting Skills

Job-hunting requires skills that most of us aren't good at. Some people have a natural ability to sell themselves but most of us have to work at it. I've read resumes for a wide spectrum of positions, from entry-level to advanced professional positions and many had serious problems and most failed to get my attention. I've interviewed hundreds of applicants, most of them well-educated professionals with the right professional skills who lacked the interview and presentation skills necessary to make the cut.

I've also been a candidate many times (way too much according to my wife) and I've learned that being a successful job hunter requires a different set of skills than being a successful professional. You can be the very best at what you do professionally and still need to learn how to sell your abilities.

Most employers have a large group of candidates for open positions. They screen for minimum requirements like education and experience. They set up barriers to eliminate candidates. There are ways to get around these barriers, but you have to make it easy for employers to identify you as someone they need to interview. Employers have three requirements for successful candidates. They're looking for people who:

Meet Their Needs

Employers usually know what they are looking for. An accounting position requires an accountant. A sales position is usually filled by a salesman. One of the most important things you learn from a job post is a company's perceptions of what their needs are. Use that knowledge to convince them that you meet their basic needs.

Add Value

Once an employer has a group of qualified candidates they hope to hit the jackpot and find an employee who exceeds expectations, makes them money, solves problems for them—or does all three. You need to focus on selling your value; convincing an employer that you not only meet their minimum requirements, but that you will solve problems and make the decision-makers look brilliant for hiring you!

Are Low-Risk

Employers want to avoid hidden landmines – employees who are dishonest, don't show up, create conflict or destroy customer relationships. Almost every employer has horror stories about hiring mistakes. You need to demonstrate that it will not be a mistake to hire you. That you get along with others, can do the job and won't be a problem. That you're low-risk.

Never forget that an employer is hiring to fill a need. Selling yourself is only marginally about you—and almost completely about the employer's needs and the benefit of bringing you on board. Your full-time job is to sell your ability to meet needs, exceed expectations by adding value and that hiring you is low risk.

Getting hired requires a skill set you can learn if you'll practice and work outside your comfort zone, but only if you make it the focus of what you do ALL THE TIME. Seize the moment, take control and employ yourself. Be your own boss and make it your job, your passion and your life to get the position you want.

YOUR PERFECT JOB

"Twenty years from now you will be more disappointed by the things you didn't do than by the ones you did do. So throw off the bowlines. Sail away from the safe harbor. Catch the trade winds in your sails. Explore. Dream. Discover." Mark Twain

You're unemployed or under-employed. Good for you . . . the future is wide open!

As long as you have so many possibilities, why not try to find a job that makes it exciting to get up in the morning? If you hated your last job and all you're trying to do is replace it, you won't be very motivated to find a new one. If you're making sacrifices to survive and searching full-time why not search for the best job you've ever had? You may not find the perfect job—but it's not that much harder to find a great job than it is it to find a lousy one.

So here's the question only you can answer—what is your perfect job? What do you want to be doing? What problems do you want to solve? What are you good at? What work do you enjoy? You have to answer these questions because where and how you look is determined by what you're looking for. Defining and looking for a great job will get you more excited about the process and help you handle rejection.

Some people will do anything to avoid being rejected—socially or professionally. Most people stay away from sales because of the full-time rejection. Job hunting—selling you—can be even worse because the rejection is personal. So you look for jobs in ways that makes the rejection less personal, like sending out lots of resumes to blind posts and applying for positions you're over-qualified for.

Get over it. When you're looking for a job you have to make a sale—but the good news is that you only have to make one sale. You need one acceptable offer. So take out a piece of paper and write down what your perfect work day looks like. Where do you live and what time do you go in? What kind of work would it need to be for you to be excited to get there early and leave late? Who do you work for and with? What impact are you having on your customers, your peers and your community? For more questions you can ask yourself go to **Appendix 1** and create the job you want to find.

Aim high. Imagine your dream job. Create a target that excites you and motivates you to keep looking no matter how bad it gets in the short term. Having a great target job will inspire you, keep you going and help you be better prepared when you get there.

NETWORKING

A good network is the best way to find a job. But in spite all of the books you've collected and programs you've attended about networking and how important it is, if you're like most people you have poor networking skills and a mediocre network. We all have address books and contacts but we don't have enough relationships with people we're comfortable asking for help finding a job. Relationships have to be built before you need them and it's hard to start building a network when you need one; especially if it's clear that you're "networking" for a job.

What's a Network?
A network is a group of people who are connected by their willingness and ability to help each other. The difference between address books, website friends, mailing lists and your network is the level and value of the relationships and your credibility with the people you know. That doesn't mean the people on your contact list can't help you, you still want to send them resumes, but without a relationship sending a resume to an acquaintance is only slightly more useful than sending it to a stranger who has a position to fill!

Your Network
Go through your address book and make a list of the people who:
- You helped find work;
- You were a reference for;
- You helped on projects or solve problems;
- You provided substantial information to—you were a reference or expert for them;
- You talk to on a regular basis;
- Know you by reputation;
- Know what you do and how well you do it.
- Your friends; and,
- Your family and in-laws (always motivated to help you find work!).

This is your network. If it's not a long list or if it doesn't include people who can help you find a job, your network isn't going to be a big help in your current job search.

Your network is where your job search starts. Contact everyone on your list. Let them know that you're looking for work and what kind of work. Ask them to review your resume and help you practice interviewing. Offer to take them to lunch for a chance to pick their brains about people they know who can help you—being referred by a mutual friend is a great way to get in the door. Continue to develop your network by offering to do the same for them or for people they know.

Build a Network

What do you do if you don't have a network? Contacting people because you need a job makes you a salesman, not a networker. Most networking activities are really prospecting socials—collecting names and phone numbers does not create a network.

Building a network takes time and hopefully you'll be able to find a job in less time that it takes to build a good network. But if you're currently unemployed, you have time. Start learning how to network today.

Your Network Trusts You. The key to building a network is to develop credibility by being a resource, building relationships and earning a good reputation. If you just get business cards, names or phone numbers, you don't have any extra credibility. People don't know who you are or what you can do; and until they do they're not really part of a meaningful network.

Talk to People. The most basic networking skill is the ability to meet and talk to people. The way to meet people and develop relationships is to talk about something that interests them—usually themselves. If you want to be a brilliant conversationalist the first thing you need to do is to listen. Be casual. I know that this sounds counter-productive, but don't talk about your job search unless it's in response to a direct question. Look for things you have in common and build connections. Take notes and build a database with information that will help you remember who people are and what they're about.

Make Real Connections. Don't mistake online "networking" for real networking. Being someone's online "friend" or creating a link is not a network. The ease of creating these connections means that no credibility is created. These sites can be great for reconnecting to people you haven't seen in a while, but after years of not talking to someone, online links probably won't be a big help in finding work.

Go Where the People Are. Building a network is a full contact sport. If you want to meet people you have to go where the people are. I belong to a number of organizations and I can tell you from experience that most people in organizations can spot job hunters (and salesmen) immediately. If you join a professional organization—Toastmasters, Rotary or the Optimists Club—make sure you stay awhile, volunteer to participate and actually become engaged before worrying about building a network or finding a job. Don't go just because you want a job. Of course, it doesn't make a lot of sense to join a group that caters to retirees when you need to meet professionals who are still working.

Share Your Skills. Don't focus on getting something back from your growing network right away. When you join a group, get involved by giving presentations, training or being a mentor. Teach the skills you're developing in your job search: developing resumes, interviewing and personal marketing. As you develop these skills, find people to share them with. Offer to interview others for practice. You'll be amazed how much you can learn when you trade seats and interview someone else or help them prepare a resume. It'll open your eyes and make your resume and interviews better.

When you find jobs you're not qualified for or can't pursue, think of who you know that may be looking for that job. Pass on the information as quickly as possible. One on the best ways to build a job-hunting network is help other people find jobs. Go out of your way to help others.

Think Long Term. A network takes time to build. Relationships require investment and an instant network probably won't appear. Networking skills are important for your whole career. Building relationships will help you in your professional and personal development, even after you have a job.

Join Existing Networks. Sometimes it's possible to benefit from someone else's network or contacts right now. Close friends with great networks and great reputations are worth their weight in gold if they'll help you make connections and recommend you to others.

If someone you know is willing to endorse you and introduce you to their friends and network this can be a great way to build credibility. Just make sure that you live up to your responsibility, which is to be trustworthy and professional. A great way to destroy a friendship is to be recommended for a job or get a reference and then blow it.

Most people who go to job fairs or groups are not networking—they're prospecting. There's a difference. Your network consists of the people who know you and trust you. Prospects are the people you meet who could be potential employers, or who can help you find an employer. With a network you have a relationship that brings you credibility. With a prospect you have to develop credibility because they don't know you at all.

Your network is made up of the people who trust you without needing a sales pitch or references. The reason that networks are such an effective way to find a job is that decision-makers like to hire people they trusted before they became a job applicant—before they wanted something. If you don't have a great network, start building one. Even if your network doesn't help you find a job this time there may be a next time or even better opportunities waiting in the future. So create a group of people who know you, who trust you, who value what you can do and what you've done.

Marketing Yourself

Jobs are everywhere; but finding and getting access to decision-makers can be frustrating and difficult.

Why is it so hard for job seekers to find employers who are looking? It's the problem that every seller has—how do you locate potential buyers and convince them to buy what you're selling.

Whether you're a company selling cars or a lawyer looking for clients the sales process is the same: find prospective customers, develop credibility, overcome objections and get a commitment.

Companies spend billions of dollars every year trying to get potential customers to try their products or take a test drive. When you're job hunting, you're the seller and most of your efforts should be aimed at identifying buyers (employers) and getting them to interview you—the job hunters equivalent of a test drive.

Your buyers have limited open positions and lots of applicants. Like any buyer, employers try to eliminate the candidates who don't fit their criteria. For each job opening an employer is going to make only one purchase and the decision-makers know that hiring decisions can have an impact on company performance and profitability for years. Most employers are so concerned about making a bad decision that their last choice for filling an opening is going to the open market and hiring someone they don't know. As a result, most positions are filled internally or by word of mouth and only a few are posted to the job-hunting population or filled by unknown candidates—less than ten percent by most estimates.

When a position is posted and there are multiple applicants, the employer has to get the number of candidates down to a workable number by eliminating people. If a hundred people apply, an employer tries to identify the five to ten people who appear to best meet the qualifications. As a seller you need to have a marketing campaign that gets you through this process of elimination.

Even if a company isn't actively looking to fill a position, they might hire you if you can convince them that you'd add value, solve a problem or can make them money. Even companies that are laying people off will hire if they have a good enough reason. Companies need good people and can't survive without them.

Your job is to find the decision-makers at companies that need you. Some of them are looking for you, most of them are not. To be successful you only need to make one sale. Understand the process and prepare yourself as best as you can. Develop a marketing strategy and work it hard.

Your Marketing Strategy

Marketing yourself is the process of creating a message and a strategy for getting the message out. It's about getting the word out that you're available to solve problems, make a difference and have an impact. Having a message—with a theme and stories—helps people understand who you are, what you do and how valuable you are!

To effectively market yourself, you have to understand what you're selling.

- What is it that you do?
- What problems do you solve?
- What value do you add?
- Why should a company hire you?

Marketing is about knowing the answer to these questions and preparing a message so you can help decision-makers understand immediately what the answers are. It's your job to make these answers clear and easy to understand.

You need to develop both a marketing strategy and tools to help you. Marketing tools are the themes, scripts and documents you create that sell you and your skills. Not only will these tools help you by providing them to employers; you'll also benefit from the process of developing them when you interview and network.

Key Message

Create a key message about yourself. A key message explains in thirty seconds:

1) Who you are;
2) What you do; and
3) The value you represent.

In sales, the key message is called an "elevator speech." What would you say to a potential employer if you found yourself in an elevator together and you only have seconds to introduce yourself?

The message has to be short, it needs to be informative and it needs to *appeal to the listener*. It should be the essence of the services you provide and the problems you solve.

When asked what they do, most people answer that they are a salesman, an engineer, or a manager—they describe themselves with the title on their business card. When you tell someone that you're a salesman, you allow them to define what a salesman is and does; you become just a salesman, just another engineer or just another manager.

Your key message allows you to define who you are and what you can do. Don't use titles. Don't use professional labels or professional lingo. Be ready to talk about what you do in terms of how it will help a potential employer. For example:

"Hello, I'm Frank and I manage customer relationships for outstanding companies. I'm an expert at developing, growing and managing customer experiences and solving customers' problems. I've managed multimillion-dollar relationships vital to my company's profit and growth. I solve customer relationship problems. I'd appreciate the chance to show you what I can do for ABC Company."

Or,

"My name is Jane, and I lead successful, profitable projects, and you're in luck because I'm looking to join a great company like yours. I managed three of my last company's most profitable projects. I identify, plan and implement successful management and technology projects. I believe in focusing on projects and strategies that make an immediate impact on the profitability and performance of an organization. Can I contact you to provide my resume and tell you how I can help your company?"

A successful key message is concise. It's persuasive, because it speaks to their needs, not yours. It explains the value you represent. And it asks for permission to make a contact.

Always ask for what you want—permission to contact them or the name of the person you should contact. Prepare your message in advance and practice it. Practice making it sound spontaneous; which means slowly, calmly, looking the recipient in the eye and prepared to answer questions. Anticipate questions, practice asking for permission to contact them or for the name of the person you should contact.

Will people shut you down? Sometimes. Some managers only pay lip service to wanting outgoing employees who show initiative. But if you meet someone who asks what you can do or what you are looking for and you don't know how to answer, you'll blow it. If you don't talk to them at all they probably won't call you! Always be prepared to market yourself.

A Sales Pitch

A sales pitch is a fifteen-minute presentation that sells you. It's your basic script for an interview or anytime you're given the chance to talk about yourself. You use your pitch when you ask decision-makers to meet you; when they don't know they need you and aren't ready to interview you. Having a prepared pitch also helps you stay on message and answer questions in interviews.

If you want to see a good sales pitch, invite a vacuum salesman or home improvement sales professional to your home. These salesmen will show up with samples, mockups, brochures and books. They'll explain how awful your life is without their product. They create a need you didn't even know you had. That's the purpose of a sales pitch.

Something I've advised people to do is actually prepare a PowerPoint presentation of their pitch, with graphics and pictures. You wouldn't use it in an interview, but preparing a visual presentation will help you organize your thoughts and remember the pitch.

A sales pitch is prepared, practiced and aimed at the customer. Your sales pitch needs to accomplish three things: build credibility, demonstrate value and create a need. You build credibility with your resume, recognizable titles and achievements and by using specific measures of success. You demonstrate value by telling *short* stories about your major accomplishments and encouraging discussions about their problems, issues and needs. And you create a need by explaining how you'll solve their problems or make them more profitable.

In a sales pitch, you take the lead. You have a script and your goal is to get questions. Get the potential buyer involved in the process and thinking about how you can solve their problems.

Here's an outline of a Sales Pitch:

1. Get the decision-maker's attention. In no more than three-to-five minutes, introduce yourself: Where you went to school, where you've worked and who you know that they might know.
2. Start with your best pitch—your biggest accomplishment or toughest problem solved. Use that story to illustrate the problems you fix, the value you add and what you can do for someone new.
3. Encourage questions about your stories. The best questions or comments are about similar issues from the employer. Focus on the employer's concerns and problems.
4. Use no more than three examples. If you have agreed to a time limit, keep to it. If your pitch goes longer than fifteen minutes, it should be their fault, not yours.
5. Let them know why you're there—you're looking to help their company as a future employee.

The best thing that can happen when you're making a pitch is to have the potential employer identify a problem you can solve. If you can start talking about how to solve *their* problems now, you'll make an impression and create a need and value.

A great pitch shouldn't be longer than fifteen minutes. If it goes longer because of their questions, great, but *you* shouldn't go longer! Practice giving your pitch in 15 minutes.

A Resume

The foundation of your marketing material is a great resume, either your model resume which is aimed at your dream job, or an employer-tailored resume created for a specific company or opening. Your resume is a marketing brochure. Be creative in how you prepare it for the audience it's aimed at. It describes all of the wonderful things you can do and have done. It demonstrates your skills and how you obtained them. You should always carry a copy of your model resume with you so that you can hand it out.

References

References can be an effective marketing tool, especially if you can get a letter of recommendation from your last manager or a senior executive who knows you well. One of the best ways to get a great letter is to write it yourself then ask your manager to sign it. E-mailing or sending copies of letters of reference is a great follow-up after an interview. They're also a great resource to put on a website.

Work Product Summaries

Use your work product to sell yourself. Good examples of the kinds of materials you can use include articles, research reports, summaries of special projects, commendations, or praise received from past employers or customers. One of the best summaries I've seen was a brochure describing a significant project a candidate had led. In it she copied e-mails from management and the client that praised the project results and her leadership. The brochure was two pages long and did a great job of showcasing her project and management skills.

Extra Materials

What if you do work that doesn't lend itself to reports or brochures? You can still find ways to showcase your skills—it just may take a little creativity. I have a friend who manages parks and recreation facilities for cities. He compiled a journal of improvements, accomplishments, and publicity related to the projects under his management. His journal showed how he was able to add value, and it set him apart. In addition, the information, articles and photos made a good resource for a website that he developed for his search.

Websites

Websites are billboards for job searchers. With a little work and minimal investment, you can create a website that highlights your accomplishments and abilities.

Just having a website doesn't ensure that the right people will look at it or that they'll like it. Creating a professional looking site can be hard, so if you have a website make sure it looks good. You also can't control who looks at your website or why—so don't use personal information that could be used for other purposes.

A website can be a great place for articles you've written, or other visual works or presentations you've created. One candidate I know created a website and posted a video of a presentation he'd given at a national conference.

Use your website as a supplement to your other marketing material. Use a generic site name and direct employers there through your resume and interviews. Don't expect an employer to find your website and call you for an interview.

Become an Expert

One of the purposes of marketing is to create name recognition and credibility. A great way to do this is to engage in activities that help you become an expert in your field. Things you can do to build your reputation include writing articles, consulting, teaching classes, leading certification groups or giving presentations in and outside your industry. If you aren't already doing these things, start now. If you get a job next week you can still continue to develop your professional reputation; it never hurts to be known as an expert.

Using marketing strategy and tools is an important part of your job search. It's how you promote yourself, set yourself apart from other candidates, build credibility and make it easier to remember who you are and what you can do. Make sure your marketing strategy helps potential employers know the value you'll bring and the problems you can solve. Spend time thinking about your story—who you are, what you do and the value you create.

WHERE TO LOOK

Where do you look for work? You look wherever employers need you to solve their problems.

Here are some ideas of how you can find potential employers and get through to the decision-makers:

Friends and Family

Family and people who really like you are the best source of leads and interviews. Get your friends and family involved in your search. Have them introduce you to people they know. Try to become more involved with their networks and expand your own circle of contacts. You'll be amazed who your friends know and how effective an enthusiastic reference can be.

Close friends in your field or profession are especially valuable contacts. Not only do they share professional experience, but they want you to succeed. Stay in touch with these friends and go out of your way to be a resource for them.

If you get an introduction from a friend or an associate, your odds of getting an interview go way up, and you bring credibility from your relationship. It takes far fewer resumes and interviews to get a job when you're referred by someone the decision-maker knows.

Networking

Networking, or who you know, is the most common way jobs are filled. An employer's greatest fear is hiring and investing in someone who doesn't work out, or worse, someone who actually damages the organization. Referrals take some of the risk out of a new hire. Decision-makers like finding someone they've heard of, someone who is referred to them or who has a good reputation in an industry. It's such an important tool that it has its own chapter—go back and read it.

Be smart when networking. Don't be pushy with people you haven't seen in a while, and don't include people who don't like you. Years ago, someone who had worked for me contacted me wanting a reference. I politely declined. We hadn't gotten along, and I wouldn't recommend him for a position. A couple of years later I interviewed an applicant and had a similar experience when one of his references had nothing good to say about him. Just because you have a name and phone number doesn't mean the person is going to help you.

Cold Calls

Cold-calling businesses for a job is hard work. Most job hunters are reluctant to call managers they don't know. But if you have a system and work at it a sales call strategy can be one of the best ways to find a great job.

An effective cold call strategy requires a process for finding prospects, setting up appointments and making a sales pitch. A process that might include the following steps.

1. Identify companies that might be interested in hiring you. Business directories available on-line or at your library can help you find companies to contact.
2. Call the companies, ask for the manager's name in the department or area you want to contact—explain that you want to send marketing information to his or her attention. If you're asked what type of information, explain that you have personal marketing information to send. Don't be afraid to call back later (a week later, not an hour) if you can't get this information on your first call.
3. Send out three, short (one-page) resumes every day with a cover letter describing your value to the managers you've identified. You could send more, but after a week, you'll be busy enough preparing resumes and cover letters, making calls and setting up appointments. If you try to do more than three a day, you run the risk of contacts falling through the cracks.
4. Five business days after sending your resume and cover letter, call the managers, follow up on the letter you sent and ask for a 15-minute appointment to introduce yourself.
5. Prepare a 15-minute sales pitch describing you, your experience and how you will add value to their company. See the chapter on **Marketing Tools** for help on putting together a

sales pitch. Bring a longer resume and other marketing material to leave at the appointment.
6. Show up on time. Give your pitch and introduce yourself. Try to get questions or discuss issues important to the manager. Ask if they need your skills and if they don't, ask if the manager knows someone else in the company you can talk to.
6. Three business days after your meeting send a follow-up letter thanking them for the meeting. Include a letter of recommendation or other information that will remind the manager who you are and what you can do.
7. Five business days after sending the follow-up letter, call the manager and ask if they have any questions or interest in hiring you. If they're interested, ask what needs to be done next. If there's no interest ask if the manager knows anyone else in the company or at another company that you can contact. If the manager provides names, request permission to use him or her as a reference.
8. Track everything. Use a spreadsheet or database to keep track of every business you contact, every resume you send and all your conversations. Keep copies of the resumes and cover letters you send to each company.

Cold calling is an incredibly effective way to find a job. You have to be consistent in sending out resumes every day, making the calls, staying organized and getting appointments. You'll be rejected, don't take it personally.

For more on cold-calling see **Rob's Story** on page 43.

Lunch

Another technique I've used is to find potential employers is to call or email a manager and invite them to lunch. Introduce yourself, explain that you're looking for a position, that you know them by reputation and that you'd like to meet them and talk to them.

Your goal at lunch is to introduce yourself, talk about the value you create and, most importantly, to learn about the manager, his company and the industry. Don't limit the conversation to just the manager's company. Try to get insights— or better yet, names of people you can contact.

When you're meeting someone for the first time, there's no context or relationship for the meeting, so try to make it about the other person, their company and their problems. Talk about their issues and offer your expertise—even if you don't get an interview. Don't make the mistake of trying to interview for a job during lunch. You can't start interviewing until you're invited to.

Recruiters

Recruiters, or headhunters, can be a great resource if you're the best candidate they have for a position. Recruiters provide relationships with decision-makers and knowledge about organizations and people. In some cases recruiters will have exclusive access to a position, but usually positions are non-exclusive, meaning they could be posted elsewhere or that other recruiters are finding candidates for the same position.

A recruiter sells employees. He or she provides a valuable service to employers by screening candidates and providing a workable pool of qualified candidates. Recruiters can provide great advice on resumes and interviewing, and help you negotiate a final deal. If a recruiter is excited about working with you then he or she is a valuable resource.

However, you can't rely on a headhunter if you don't have a good relationship. If you're qualified but the headhunter isn't excited about you they can become another barrier to getting an interview. A couple of years ago, a recruiter told me that I was his primary candidate for a position. I was a little surprised that I never had a phone interview. I later found out that my resume never reached the company. I assume I wasn't the recruiter's first choice and that he didn't want me competing for the job. I never worked with him again.

I've learned other things in working with recruiters. Recruiters sometimes post positions that don't exist. They're fishing for product (you) and want to build their resume database. Always ask for the company name when applying for a position.

Sometimes you're a B list candidate; there's another candidate who the recruiter thinks is more qualified and you're submitted to make him or her look better. It's okay to occasionally be the back-up, but don't let yourself be used that way all the time. Make sure the recruiter submits you as the A list candidate for the right jobs.

Sometimes recruiters submit resumes to employers without asking for permission. When you start working with a recruiter confirm in writing (e-mail will do) that he or she won't submit your resume without your permission.

Also avoid using recruiters who charge for their help. Most of what they provide you can do yourself. If a fee seems like a good investment, make it contingent on actually getting a job at a specific salary.

I'm not against working with recruiters; I've gotten great interviews working with great professional recruiters. They are an important part of a good strategy if you remember a few things.

- Find recruiters you like and that are excited to be working with you.
- Don't work with more than two or three recruiters at a time and avoid working with recruiters who tend to be looking to fill the same positions and represent the same companies.
- Keep in touch with them—once a week if you've been presented for position, at least once a month if there are no active applications.
- If a recruiter makes a recommendation, follow it. If they want you to change your resume, do it. If there are resources or coaching available, use them.
- Don't be afraid to interview recruiters. If one doesn't get back to you, isn't excited to work with you or doesn't have positions, find another one.

Job Fairs

Job fairs are a good place to find prospects, practice interview and speaking skills and learn more about local employers. The downside is that most job fairs focus on entry-level positions and the decision-makers aren't there. The HR reps who attend aren't usually looking to fill specific positions and if they are, it might be because of high turnover in less desirable positions.

You can develop a successful job fair strategy by knowing which employers are going to be at a fair and what types of positions they need to fill. Job fairs often have websites that list participating employers. Dress and act like you're interviewing the whole time you're at the fair. Have a key message—who you are and the value you create—that you can give in thirty seconds. Get lots of names and business cards and distribute your resume and marketing material. Take notes as you meet people. You won't usually get a job at a job fair, but you can get contacts, resources and leads.

Internet

The internet has replaced the newspaper for job posts. It is where many of your competitors (other job seekers) will begin and end their search.

Online job sites and postings are the *most* popular but *least* effective way to find a new job! Candidates can't distinguish themselves on the internet. Resumes submitted in electronic format all look the same. There's no way to build credibility, which is essential in the hiring process.

The internet is a great tool for doing research about companies and people. It can lead you to organizations that are hiring. But it's *not* a great way to find a new job. Most jobs are not posted. I know from experience that many of the positions on the internet are filled by internal candidates or known outsiders through a relationship, a reference or by reputation.

If a job is posted it doesn't mean there isn't an internal candidate for the position already. Sometimes a manager knows who they want to hire but is required to interview other candidates. It's a bummer, but there are times when your interview just helps an employer complete his checklist before hiring a friend.

When companies post positions on popular job sites they get more resumes than they want. Over half are completely unqualified or so poorly written that they're immediately rejected. The rest are quickly reviewed to identify the most likely candidates. Employers have learned that few good applicants come from internet posts so they eliminate almost all of them, especially if they have other options.

People do get hired from the internet, but the odds aren't good. Go ahead and apply to internet posts—but don't rely on them to find a job. Keep track of how often you find jobs on each site that you respond to. Quit looking at services or job boards that never have positions that you're interested in or that apply to you.

Company websites are a valuable resource. Looking at posted positions you can learn their general requirements. Use company sites to figure out who the hiring managers are if you can—bigger companies hide this information as if it's top secret! Apply on the company website, but always follow up with a paper resume and cover letter.

Avoid spending all your time searching the internet. Don't search sites every day (or several times a day). As a general rule, no more than twenty percent of your time should be spent on the internet looking at job services and responding to posts. Make a list of sites you need to check and companies you want to keep track of and set up a schedule. Company job sites probably don't need to be looked at more than once a week.

Marketing

Marketing—the "build it and they will hire you" model—is putting the word out that you are looking for a job and then waiting for employers to find you. Unless you're a marketing professional or want to spend money on a billboard, this probably shouldn't be a major part of your strategy. The biggest problem with this method is that most employers simply aren't looking – they don't have to.

The two most common forms of personal marketing today are putting your resume on a website and developing a personal website designed to showcase your job search and abilities.

It's easy to put your resume on a job site. But it's unlikely that anyone is searching the hundreds of thousands of such resumes. Remember that a resume includes a lot of personal information that can be used for other purposes.

A personal website can help you get noticed or demonstrate your skills in computer or technical fields—*if* you use your resume to direct employers there. Make sure that your job marketing website (www.hirejsmith.com) reflects the image you're trying to present. Take the time to also make sure that personal or family websites, blogs and networking sites are appropriate and consistent; read the chapter on **Your Image**. A marketing website might not help you get a job, but inappropriate information about you on the internet can definitely keep you from getting an offer.

Using a website can be a way to distinguish yourself in a competitive market, but don't rely on just a marketing approach and don't spend a lot of money or time on these kinds of projects.

Coming up with a job search strategy is a function of what you know, what you can do and who you know that can help you get the message out. No matter what your strategy is, you'll face rejection. Getting a job—making that one sale—is a numbers game where the numbers get bigger when the economy is bad. So play the odds and create multiple ways for employers to find you.

Mixing strategies will give you the best odds of getting a job. The secret is to look everywhere and to try everything that makes sense, doesn't cost a lot of money and is professional. It takes a lot of work.

Much of what you try won't be successful. It would be great if your first resume nets a quick first interview and a lucrative job offer. This isn't reality for most of us—it takes time, patience and perseverance to get your target job. But you can do it if you have a plan, if you work your plan and if you don't give up.

Boundaries

In most job searches, we set boundaries that define our search and the kind of job we're looking for. These boundaries are created by our experience, degrees, titles and expectations. Too often the kind of job we look for is similar to the one we just had. And our last job is just a more advanced version of the first real job we got out of school. One of the things you have to do is question the boundaries of your search and the pre-conceptions about what you do for a living, how you do it and where you work.

If you stay inside your preset boundaries you limit your options. You may end up competing with more people for fewer jobs and it'll take more time to find one. By expanding your boundaries and looking for other opportunities to use your skills you create new options and increase your chance of success.

Titles

The first boundary for many people is a title that narrowly defines what they do. Some people with very general skills such as sales or office management have spent years in a specific niche and look for the same title in the same niche when they hunt for a new job. The more you limit the definition of your career, the harder it is to find a replacement job. That's why you need to spend time describing the types of problems you solve and the skills you have. It's your skills that will open doors and allow you to be a candidate for positions you might not have thought of exploring before.

For example, in the insurance industry handling claims and underwriting policies are two very different career paths. Usually people on one side of the business don't go to the other. Yet if you review the skills, knowledge and experience needed for these career paths they have many more similarities than differences. Very few claim professionals apply for underwriting positions or vice-versa; but a prospective employee could sell him or herself as an insurance professional and dramatically expand the jobs that are available.

If you believe you have the skills and can legitimately do a job, go ahead and apply for it. Use your cover letter and resume to demonstrate that you're qualified even if you don't have the title or years of experience. You'll be rejected by some employers—maybe even most of them. You'll have to be perfect in the interviews. But don't eliminate yourself by not applying for a position if you believe you can do or learn it.

Career Field

The same is true for moving to a new career. By focusing on your skills and results it's possible make a jump to a completely different industry if you are willing to research new positions and educate yourself. It'll take more resumes and more interviews to get a job, but if you don't apply for these opportunities you have no chance of of getting an interview and no chance of getting hired.

So why don't more people make the jump from one career path or industry to another? The primary reason is perceptions and self-imposed boundaries. We're part of a group and we identify with that group. We don't even think about looking at opportunities with other groups. In some cases, we actually have emotional responses to moving to another career path within the same industry. People develop a team mentality, so other career paths are seen as the other team . . . one we would never join.

Another valid reason is that it's harder to find a job in another field. You have preconceptions; decision-makers do too. You'll be rejected more often when you try to make a significant career change. Screeners will filter you out and you'll have to make more of an effort to get to the decision-makers. Your best chance to make a significant change, and the most common way it occurs, is through people who know you and are willing to take a chance. But that doesn't mean it doesn't happen or that you shouldn't broaden the scope of your search.

In fact, it can be liberating to pursue a position in an unrelated field. On several occasions I've tracked down hiring managers and bypassed HR department. Some managers were annoyed, but I've interviewed several times in unrelated fields and enjoyed the process (although I never got a job offer).

Another reason most people don't make the switch to a new career field is that the more significant the change the more likely it is that you'll have to take a pay cut. In some cases, you may have to take a couple of steps backwards. Whether you want to do that is something you'll have to decide. But if the industry you want to move to is a growth industry and appears to be more stable in the future than the industry you're leaving, taking a step back for a couple of years can make sense.

Geography

A significant boundary people encounter is geographic location. It's okay to have guidelines and preferences on where you're willing to move and the areas of the country where you'll work. But if you aren't willing to relocate at all then your choices are significantly limited—especially if there are few options where you live. To have the best chance of finding new employment you need to be flexible in where you're willing to live.

Moving can be difficult for a family and complicated when a spouse has a job that will be hard to replace. But limiting yourself to a specific location will decrease your options and could significantly increase the time it takes to get your professional career back on track.

Sometime there are limitations you can't overcome. If you haven't been to medical school you probably shouldn't apply for medical positions. The same is true of most jobs that require specific education or a license. But most of the boundaries that limit us are self-imposed. An employer wants a job done and a problem solved. Market your ability to solve problems regardless of title, industry or location. Don't take yourself out of the running before you even apply—let employers make a decision whether or not to interview you. When you interview for these positions, sell your ability to think outside the box and solve new and exciting problems.

BE CONFIDENT

It was a tough decision whether to name this chapter "Be Confident," or "Don't Be Desperate."

"Be Confident" won out, it's more positive and on target—but the end result is the same. No matter how bad things get, no matter how depressed you are, no matter how desperate you may feel you can't let it show or let that become the motivation for what you do and how you do it.

Desperation, a close cousin to panic, leads to bad decisions. Confidence brings clarity, allows you to evaluate your options and helps you convey your ability to solve problems and add value.

Years ago I was interviewing an applicant for a professional position. He had the experience and skills I wanted, but he avoided my eyes during introductions. I handed him a list of questions and asked him to answer them. Within minutes he was rambling, telling me about his problems and significant personal failures. Based on his resume and experience he was a decent candidate, but he was desperate. He didn't expect to get the job, so he didn't come prepared to convince me that he could help solve *my* problems—which would have solved a lot of his problems.

If you get an interview, be confident that you can get the job, that you can do the job and that you're going to do great in the interview.

Stay Positive

There are many emotional responses to the problems that come with being unemployed or looking for a better job. Anger, fear, doubt, shame, powerlessness, frustration, and cynicism are all likely.

Negative emotions are re-enforced when you're rejected, and those feelings start to define how you see yourself. Instead of feeling frustration with your circumstances you begin to see yourself and your abilities in a negative way, believing that you're flawed.

Don't give in to negative responses. You have to resist negative self-talk and self-labeling because it will have a significant impact on your motivation and ability to look for a job.

In addition, negative emotional assumptions are mostly untrue. Our responses are usually based are false assumptions about other people's motivations or conclusions about us. We get angry because we assume that what others are doing and saying is personal. We got tough questions because they didn't like us from the beginning. We did poorly in an interview because we're incapable.

These conclusions are usually not true. The vast majority of applicants are not rejected because they have a personal deficiency and you're not a loser. We all have good days and bad days; we have good interviews and bad interviews. The only way to lose is to quit trying. Whether you keep trying is completely in your control.

But what if it really is personal? What if the person who fired or rejects you is the biggest jerk in the world? What if a rejection letter actually said, "We have determined that you are the biggest loser we have ever interviewed." So what?! You could get angry, frustrated or depressed. But what would that accomplish? Move on, leave the idiots without the benefit of your skills and keep going. You have the ability to decide how to react.

Emotions are natural and most of our emotional responses are learned. They can be unlearned. Think back to the kinds of things that made you mad in school. Hopefully you can laugh about the insults and problems that set you off back then. Over time, you've learned not to get upset about high school insults. Unfortunately, you've learned since then to get upset about a new group of issues.

How do you overcome negative reactions? Through discipline, self-examination and practice. When you begin to indulge in negativity, recognize it. Ask yourself why. Why do I feel this way? Is there something I need to learn from this experience, something I should change the next time I do whatever I just did? Will my response right now help me move forward? Will being depressed, frustrated or angry help me be more persuasive, interview better or get motivated to send out more resumes and look for more opportunities?

If your emotional responses aren't helping, motivating or making you better at what you need to do, get over them, quit indulging yourself and move on.

Act and Look Confident

You don't feel confident. You're nervous, and you suspect that the whole world knows it just by looking at you. How do you *act* confident? Simple: you figure out how confident people look and act—and you copy them.

For years, I've given presentations on public speaking and taught techniques to help speakers relax. Confident speakers establish eye contact. They stand on the balls of their feet. They use bigger, slower gestures, and they breathe deeply. If you can learn these behaviors you can get your body to relax when you speak.

It works even if you don't believe you're confident, even if you're sure that nobody else believes it. It's a funny thing, but if you can force yourself to act confident, your subconscious starts to believe that you *are* confident and you relax. The same techniques can work with interviewing if you know what confident interviewees do.

Confident interviewees:

- Have a firm handshake.
- Remember and use the name of the interviewer.
- Sit up straight, leaning forward to emphasize answers.
- Establish non-threatening eye contact (no staring contests) and avoid looking at the ceiling or their feet.
- Don't criticize anyone—themselves, former employers or people they don't know.
- Answer the questions that are asked; they don't ramble.
- Don't tell jokes or discuss politics (unless interviewing for a political position).
- Show they know how to listen by responding to what was said or asked.

- Remember to breathe and speak at a reasonable pace.
- Smile—it's a great way to tell your body that you're okay, so keep smiling as long as it's appropriate.

You learn these techniques by practicing them. When you practice interviewing, focus on the behaviors of a confident interviewer so you'll feel like you've been there before when you get to the final interview.

Don't Sabotage Yourself

Don't add to your problems by not looking or acting your best when you go to an interview. I thought dressing to impress was common knowledge until I helped a friend conduct interviews for a sales position. I was amazed how the candidates showed up and what they did while they were there.

Avoid extremes in dress and behavior. Use your practice interviews to identify nervous habits and fix them. Habits can distract or annoy an interviewer. They can be distracting to you when you're concerned about how you look or how you're presenting yourself.

Other thoughts from my experiences in interviewing:

- Dress professionally. Look good and you'll feel better.
- Don't wear too much perfume or cologne. Please!
- Turn off your cell phone and electronics. It's a good idea to put keys, phones and loose change in your briefcase or purse until after the interview.
- Be awake and alert.

You *can* create issues with your appearance or behavior that make the interview a failure—sometimes rightfully so.

Be Confident—Not Egotistical

An interview is a strange experience. You want to communicate your expertise, confidence and great skills—without being overbearing or silly about it. Your mission is to answer questions confidently without being overbearing.

Don't be the candidate who has to be perfect at everything, who has never made a mistake, who is insulting or dismissive of others, or whose primary qualification is their arrogance. When you're asked about your failures and weaknesses demonstrate some humility and grasp of reality by being aware of what some of your weaknesses are. You don't want to beat yourself up, but talk about what you need to improve and your plan for becoming more skilled and professional

Here are ideas to help you look and act confident, but not appear to have a raging ego:

- Don't claim to the best in the world at anything—even if you are.
- Don't brag about conquests, popularity or sexual prowess.
- Don't go out of your way to be cool, trendy or hip. Unless you're interviewing with a fashion magazine.
- Don't get upset, rude or crude with anyone in the building. Receptionists and secretaries are often asked to evaluate interactions with candidates.
- Don't act like you don't care . . . unless you really don't care.
- Listen and ask for clarification of questions or instructions.
- Follow the instructions you receive.
- Be a nice person.
- Smile.

Confidence as an interviewee comes from having a strategy, being prepared and practicing interviewing skills. Be firm, be committed, focus on your objectives and you will not only appear confident—you'll begin to *be* confident.

BURNING BRIDGES

Don't burn your bridges with people you know or the organizations you've been part of. Too often, when someone is laid off or hates a job, they attack and destroy relationships.

Here are some questions you need to answer: If you stop by your former workplace, will they be happy to see you? Did you leave in a way that might make them want to have you back? If not, why not? Sometimes you don't have any control over circumstances or bad feelings. But if you do, make an effort to make the best of a bad situation.

Getting upset is natural; lashing out, taking revenge or hurting people can burn bridges you need and destroy resources you want. You can make it impossible to go back and difficult to maintain relationships that could be important to you. Hopefully it's not too late to maintain important relationships and resources.

Be Gracious. Maybe *gracious* isn't the best way to describe it—don't lose your cool. Treat the people around you with respect and don't do anything stupid. Don't load up on office supplies or destroy company property.

Be Helpful. Finish work that needs to be done if you have the time. Make it clear that people can contact you with questions. Organize your work and files. Make the transition easy for the people who have to do your work when you're gone.

Be Professional. Let clients know what's happening and offer your services if issues come up (former clients are great future employers). Don't badmouth your employer and don't be any less professional about the organization than you were when you were happily employed.

Offer Your Services. Offer to help on a consulting basis. They're probably shorthanded and you know what needs to be done. If you can work something out, you can earn money and put yourself back in line to be hired if things change.

Ask for references. Use your managers and coworkers as a resource. Ask them to be references, or better yet, get a letter of reference for your marketing folder—but only if they like you.

Keep in touch. Hopefully there are people in your company who you want to stay in touch with. Get together or talk on the telephone. Don't be a downer when you do see each other. Be concerned about the stress in their lives. Former colleagues are a great resource for practice interviews and reviewing resumes.

Don't burn bridges or people out of frustration. Don't blame people for what happened to you—even if they deserve blame. Controlling your responses and emotions gives you more control over your life and your choices. Don't let your anger and frustration cause you to do or say things you'll regret.

If you handle it right you may be able to add your previous employer to your list of assets, not a liability you hope potential employers won't contact. You don't always have control of a situation or the circumstances surrounding a job loss, but you can control how you react. Be a class act and emotionally and strategically you'll be better prepared to find your next position.

THE DECISION-MAKER

Years ago, I had a strange experience when I interviewed for a management position. I was flown in as a top candidate after several phone interviews. When I arrived at the office early in the morning the receptionist just stared at me with open hostility, but I couldn't figure out why.

Another odd part of the interviews came when one of the interviewers let it slip that he was also being considered for the position. I'd never been interviewed by a competitor before. The rest of the day went great and I thought my interview with the company's president went really well—in fact, we talked for over an hour when we were only scheduled to talk for twenty minutes. I thought I was going to get an offer.

Two weeks later, the vice president called to tell me that I wasn't getting the job. She was professional and answered my questions about their decision (always try to get information and feedback). They had promoted the supervisor who had interviewed me. She explained that everyone who had interviewed or interacted with me was part of the decision, except for the company's president, who was out of town when they met. She told me that I was a "very strong" candidate, but the receptionist had reported that I was aloof and arrogant when I arrived. They didn't want to hire someone the receptionist thought was arrogant!

What I found out later was that the receptionist was a close friend of the supervisor and thought he should get the job. She didn't have a clue who was more qualified. Worse, she wouldn't be affected if he did a bad job. The vice president wasn't secure in her position and was concerned about how long I had talked with her boss. Apparently the whole office was watching the clock while we talked.

So what's the point of this story?

Not everyone you'll meet during the process can help you, but everyone you meet during an interview can hurt you.

Don't assume that you know who the decision-maker is. That person is not always clear—and it may not be well-defined in the company. I've been in situations where the manager deferred to someone else with a stronger opinion, or a superior weighed in at the last minute. Dynamics change all the time in a company or department so don't assume one person is *the* decision-maker. Everyone you meet will make a decision and you can't guess which ones will matter most.

Interview with Everyone

This doesn't mean every question requires a two-minute answer. When you're asked if you need your parking validated, just say yes with a smile. Just be on your best behavior from the time you park your car or get out of a cab. You don't know if people on the elevator are going to be interviewing you later. If you're rude to someone in the building it can get back to the decision-makers.

Don't talk or play games on your cell phone. Don't listen to headphones. Sit up no matter where you're sitting. Don't chew gum. Don't ask the receptionist for her phone number. Don't be informal with anyone. When you're there for an interview, be there for the interview the whole time.

Be Professional

A common mistake occurs when a candidate interviews with someone they see as an equal—someone they'll be working *with* and not *for*. Candidates sometimes feel they need to be buddies with future coworkers, so they complain about past bosses, tell funny stories and share personal experiences. Don't do it. You need to be friendly, outgoing and professional. Keep your answers short and focus on your value. When interviewing with a possible co-worker, tell them how easy you are to work with, how you like to help everyone and how you can make their life easier. When I've been part of a group interview I always voted for the one who convinced me that he or she would make my life easier.

When dealing with someone who may report to you be professional. Don't be rude or arrogant (I wasn't . . . really). Act like your favorite boss, the one who treated you like a human being. Not everyone you meet will get to vote, but stories about candidates who are jerks spread quickly.

Don't Compete

This was probably my real mistake. I was probably too interested in the vice president's job. When you're qualified to do the job of the person who's hiring you, you need to be careful to assure him or her that you'll be loyal. Loyalty is a huge issue for any manager, and more so when you're a great (or over-qualified) candidate. Don't compete for a job that's not available.

Don't try to top every story that's told. I once interviewed a candidate and casually mentioned that I was sore from riding 100 miles on a bicycle the day before. He immediately told me about his 200-mile ride; which may have been true but was mostly annoying. It quickly became clear that he had to top every story someone told. I asked the other interviewers to make up stories to see how he'd respond. By the end of the day we had a great time retelling all the stories he told us—he'd been everywhere and done everything and none of it was believable!

Even if it's true, don't try to outdo your interviewers. The interview process isn't about you—it's about helping your future employer solve a problem or fill a need. Don't compete.

I wish I knew the secret to identifying the decision-maker when you're interviewing. Even if a manager tells you he or she is the sole decision-maker, don't believe it. In High School I worked in a small electronics store. When I was hired I assumed the owner made all the decisions and had hired me. It was only after I was hired that I realized his wife had absolute veto power. She would brush by a candidate or watch him interview in the office and veto a candidate without asking a question.

Everyone you meet during interviews has a decision to make about you. The only decision you control is how you'll act and what you'll say in every interaction. Stay professional and be on top of your game with everyone you meet. So don't guess. Don't quit interviewing until you get home.

CREATING A JOB—ROB'S STORY

Remember that perfect job you're looking for? The one that gets you excited about getting up every day and makes rejection easier to handle! Your chances of finding and getting hired for that perfect job from help-wanted ads or internet posts are about the same as getting hit by lightning and winning the lottery in the same week (I don't know the exact odds—but you get the idea).

That's the bad news . . . the good news is that you can create your perfect job.

This is really Rob's story. Rob is a friend who, after six difficult and challenging months of looking for a job through posts and networking had gotten just a few interviews and no offers. He was about to lose hope when he learned how to sell himself and got three offers in two weeks. All of them were a move up and the job he accepted is exactly what he was looking for.

Rob is typical of many people looking for a job today. He has a two-year degree in engineering. He's been a product manager with significant responsibilities and twenty years of management experience. He interviewed for his first position right out of college and never had to look for a job because all his new jobs came from friends and colleagues; until he was laid off in a bad economy. He was unprepared to be a job hunter. He'd never thought about creating a network. His Associates Degree turned out to be an issue when applying for jobs where he was unknown. After soul searching, prayer, and some inspired advice, this is what he learned.

First, he had to sell himself. To start, he investigated who his market was. He worked at the library for a few hours each week using business directories to identify all of the local businesses in the same categories as his previous employers. To his surprise, there were hundreds of potential employers.

Next, he went to the internet and researched the companies he wanted to contact. He called the companies and asked for the name of the senior manager or executive in charge of product development, telling the receptionist that he wanted to send information. He was never asked what kind of information he wanted to send and he always got a name. He was prepared to say he wanted to send a resume of a well-qualified engineer—but it never came up.

He sent a cover letter and short resume detailing his skills and experience. He kept track of all the cover letters and resumes in a spreadsheet for easy retrieval and within five days he called to follow up. He'd ask about their business and offered to answer questions regarding his letter and resume.

The key was sending three resumes a day, five days a week. At first it was difficult to pick up the phone and make the follow-up calls, but it became easier as he learned what to say and how to present himself. Every day he made the calls and every day he tracked the results in his spreadsheet. He didn't send more than three letters a day, because it was too difficult to research and follow up on more than three.

Most of the managers didn't want to meet with Rob, but *all* of them took a moment to talk to him. The conversations varied, but Rob's focus was on talking about what their company was doing and what their problems were. By the end of second week, he started setting up appointments. In three weeks he'd sent out almost fifty resumes.

Always prepared for the interview, Rob took with him all the information needed to fill out an application if one was asked for. Before each interview he researched that company and spent time reviewing his notes from previous conversations.

The interviews were more like sales calls than job interviews. None of the managers he met with had asked for the interview and few had openings. They agreed to an appointment but it was his job to set the agenda. So he prepared a sales pitch. He created marketing material, including a longer resume and summaries of the projects he'd managed. He started by introducing himself, his background and his specific experience. He focused on the problems he'd solved by telling stories. Managers often stopped him to ask about a similar problem they were having, giving him an opportunity to talk about how he could solve their issues. Several times, he was actually taken into the facility and was able to demonstrate his knowledge and expertise.

After the appointment he followed up with a letter, sometimes making suggestions regarding the issues they had discussed. Usually he included a letter of reference from his last employer.

After about eight weeks of full-time focus on soliciting interviews, Rob got two offers the same week. Neither job had existed before he contacted the companies. Both of these jobs were acceptable, but he had identified a third company he wanted to work for. He called this company, his favorite, one last time to let them know that if they were interested they needed to act quickly. His third and best offer came within days from that company.

Rob's story is unusual only because so few people are willing to extend themselves more, get outside their comfort zone and sell themselves to employers who aren't even looking. What's not unusual is his success. In a tough job market, it may take four or five months instead of two, but there are great companies with problems you can solve. Know what you're selling, identify your potential customers, come up with a strategy—and then work at it.

You can make the sale.

Rejection

I've got bad news for you: you're going to be rejected. It's part of the job description.

- You won't receive responses to most of the resumes you send out.
- People you thought were friends will be uncomfortable or even get upset when asked to help.
- You'll perform poorly in some interviews.
- You won't make it past the first round of interviews for some jobs.
- You'll do great in all the interviews with an employer and come in second or third.

That's how it works. It's normal, it's not a conspiracy and there is only one thing you can do if you're going to get a job: KEEP GOING.

Most people give up too easily. The average job hunter sends out between twenty-five and fifty resumes. They'll interview three to four times and then stop looking. Too many wait until benefits run out to even start looking for a new job. The initial unemployment period is treated like an unexpected vacation instead of the intense job hunt that it needs to be. Studies have suggested that most people who lose their jobs stop looking after three months of casual searching—and won't start seriously looking again until they're desperate or prodded.

Wouldn't it be great if you only had to write one resume, send out a couple of them, get an interview and get an offer during the interview—and while you're at it, you'd like to be pleasantly surprised with the title, office and salary that's offered? Okay, back to reality.

Making any sale—including selling yourself—is a numbers game. There are only so many openings this week, so many companies and organizations that need someone with your skills (probably more than you know), and other people looking for every position. You're competing for these positions, and you'll lose some of the competitions—but if you know the odds and don't give up you'll win one. And that's all you need!

How many resumes you have to send out to get an interview will depend on a number of factors. Let's assume that after trial and error, you discover that it takes ten of your best resumes to get a meaningful interview. Then you discover that it takes five interviews with different companies to get to the final round, and for every three times you get to the final round you receive an offer. This means that to get a valid offer, on average you'll have to send one hundred and fifty resumes, interview with fifteen companies and be a final candidate three different times.

Some of you are thinking this sounds awful. Not so—this is great news! If you knew the exact numbers for your job search, you'd know how long your search will be and you'd know exactly what it takes to get a job. Then all you'd need to know is: how soon can you get the resumes out?

I can't tell you what the numbers are for your personal job search. The numbers are a function of the field you work in, how narrowly you limit your search, the job market, where you're willing to look for employment (geography), the strength of your resume and of you as a candidate. If you insist on staying in a specific city, looking for a specific job title with a specific type of company you'll significantly increase the number of contacts you have to make, resumes you need to send and interviews required to get an offer. Your search is going to require all of these steps, usually multiple times and rejection is not only part of the process, but a natural consequence of a successful job hunt. When you're rejected, you keep going.

So how do you stay motivated and positive during this process? Here are a few principles that help me:

Stay Focused on Your Perfect Job

Be committed to finding a job you really want. I encourage people to make their target job as big and as exciting as possible. If you hated your last job and you're looking for the same kind of position it's easy to get discouraged. Lack of money is motivation, but most people only get motivated when it's all gone, they're desperate and then they take the first job that provides a check. You can do better than that. So take the time to define your perfect job or staying motivated will be more difficult.

Don't Take Rejection Personally

People who take a pass on your resume or choose other candidates during the interview process aren't judging you personally. No employer or interviewer gets to know you in a short interview. They're trying to make the best possible decision, and it isn't personal. Even if it were—you can't take it personally. Learn from your experience and move on.

Learn from Every Experience

Every time you come out of an interview collect your thoughts, write notes and try to evaluate what went well and what did not. You might even keep a journal or notebook of your interview experiences. Was there a question that was difficult or that you didn't handle well? Write it down and work on a better answer. If you didn't feel good during the interview make a note not to eat whatever you ate the night before. If you don't think you looked the part or there was something else that didn't feel right, make note of it and come up with a strategy to improve your performance and do better the next time.

Every Rejection Gets You Closer to an Offer

There's a maxim in sales: Every "no" gets you closer to a "yes." If you knew that it will take 149 "no's" to get an offer, you could just check one more rejection off the list and keep going towards that yes.

Stay Away from the Negative People

Lots of people will tell you that you've done enough, that no one is hiring, that there are no opportunities and that it's not your fault you can't get a job. Being successful is about taking responsibility and excuses aren't acceptable. Don't listen to the media, your associates or people who mean well when they tell you to give up. Just smile, send out more perfect resumes, get invited to more interviews and prove them wrong.

Make the Decision to Be Positive

We decide how we emotionally respond to the events in our lives. We allow ourselves to get angry, either intentionally or by habit. We decide whether to be positive or negative about the events that happen because of us and to us.

Rejection is difficult to deal with. Even without adversity, it can be difficult to wake up every morning without a job, living on the edge and unsure of the future—I get that. But you really only have two choices: you can give up or you can keep going.

The good news is that if you're willing to be rejected, if you'll do the work and keep going, you'll find work. You'll be employed again. You can get through this experience stronger than you started it. Keep going until you succeed

YOUR IMAGE

You've sent out perfect resumes but you haven't gotten a bite, not even a nibble. It could just be bad luck or bad timing, but you need to make sure there aren't other obstacles getting in your way. Investigate what you're projecting to the world—your image.

Years ago, I had to hire a lawyer for my department. I identified five or six candidates to call in for interviews and asked my assistant to set up the appointments. Later that morning, she came into my office laughing. She dialed one of the hopefuls on my speakerphone so I could hear his voicemail message. The message was clever, about his recovering from a party the night before. It had specific instructions and lewd suggestions for blondes and brunettes. It was original and creative—but I didn't leave a message. I went back to the pile of resumes and picked the next best one.

Maybe I was too harsh but I'd received over a hundred resumes for one position and I didn't want to waste time trying to decide if the candidate could be professional enough for a senior position in my department. He may have made a good employee, but he made it easy for me to take a pass. Be aware of how you are projecting yourself to the world.

Make sure that your image, your messages and your reputation match your marketing pitch.

It's becoming increasingly common for employers to perform internet searches for basic information about candidates. Do one yourself before you contact an employer to make sure you know what is out there about you—or anyone with a similar name—on the internet.

Review the communities you're part of on the internet and organizations you belong to that have websites. Being part of social networks is common. Carefully review your sites, blogs and profiles to make sure that nothing embarrasses you or is inconsistent with your resume and interviews. If something doesn't reflect the right image and you can't edit the content, or get others to change their posts to your sites, seriously think about closing your accounts and profiles.

A friend once interviewed a woman who claimed she had lost her job because of staff cuts. When he found her profile on a social networking site, he found she had written several blogs about stupid employers who had fired her—including a couple of employers not on her resume. Anything on the internet is fair game for employers trying to figure out who you are.

Be careful if you've been using dating or adult-oriented websites. Employers don't usually search these websites unless image is an important part of the position being filled, but there are stories about applicants who have embarrassing profiles come up during a background check. You need to be aware of information that's available to anyone doing a search and clean it up or being prepared to deal with it. You're trying to avoid employers finding something inconsistent with your image or information that increases the risk of being rejected.

Your image is part of your marketing effort to build credibility and trust. Companies spend millions to protect and preserve reputations and appearances. You need to protect your professional image in the same way that companies want to protect their images. If you make it difficult for employers to determine that you're professional, or whether you'll protect *their* reputation, they'll usually take a pass.

Perfect Resumes

The Perfect Resume

Big confession—there is no perfect resume! A resume that gets you an interview is as perfect as a resume gets . . . If you write your name and phone number on a napkin and it gets you an interview, it's a perfect resume. There is no other purpose for a resume and no resume will guarantee an interview.

Your goal is to create the best pitch for why you should get an interview—not why you should be hired. The perfect resume sells your ability to help a potential employer, but no resume will please every employer or get past every screener. Slick-looking resumes will impress some people and turn others off. Pictures will get you some interviews and rejected for others. Sometimes screeners are having a good day and others will be having a bad day. Don't worry about the things you can't control; to be successful obsess about the things you do control!

Make sure that you're doing everything you can to make your resume as close to perfect as possible.

Edit, Edit, Edit

Edit your resume several times before other people look at it. Don't allow misspelled words. Make sure that your resume looks professional and flows well. Have it reviewed by several other people who are great at writing and listen to their advice. Print it out and edit it on paper, not just on the computer. Read it aloud. Read it backwards—last line to the first line. Keep reading it to make sure that it's not just good, but *great*.

Appearance

Appearance is important, especially for paper resumes and cover letters. There's a reason people make a living designing ads and publications—appearance impacts buying decisions. Take your resume and pin it to a wall. Back up and look at it. Does it look good? You have to get the attention of the first person who is thinning the pile of resumes. Do everything you can to create balance and a consistent style throughout the whole document, including the cover letter.

I like to use justified block text for the larger passages of text. I have a header panel that serves as a letterhead, and I use it on both the cover letter and resume. But I know there are many ways to structure the design and I'm always playing with how my resume looks. If you know someone with design experience ask them to look at your resume and help you improve it.

Avoid bold colors unless artistic ability is part of the job you're applying for. Be careful with pictures. They don't scan well into resume programs and most are not memorable or helpful. On the other hand, one of the most effective resumes I've seen included a photo of the applicant doing volunteer service in a foreign country. It was different, created interest and made it easy to remember him.

Be careful with formatting. Common errors include unusual formatting and a lack of consistency throughout a resume. If you are centering section headings (Education, Employment, etc.), make sure they're *all* centered. Avoid right-side justification for headings and information, if for no other reason than it can distract a reader trying to quickly scan the document. Italics and bold are appropriate, but use them sparingly, consistently, and in a way that doesn't distract. The goal of your formatting is to make it easier for the reader to use your resume to find the information they need.

If your resume is submitted in an electronic format and will be entered into a database, eliminate most of the formatting and focus on the quality of the text. Formatting will be lost when a resume is entered into a system. Create multiple resumes—one to submit to databases, and others for interviews or to mail to companies as follow-up.

Length

Make sure your resume is long enough to sell your experience but not so long that the length becomes a distraction. For anyone with more than three years' experience a resume should be about two pages, no longer. You want a worthwhile list of accomplishments, education and interests without overstating any aspect or making it difficult to read.

Employers don't read resumes the first time through—they glance at them. They look at the main headings, scan the small print and eliminate resumes that don't fit expectations or look right. That's why things like length and appearance are important—they convey something about the applicant right away.

If you only have a single page of personal information, don't repeat information or embellish just to get another page. If you have too much information, cut it down to two pages. If you have long lists of accomplishments like articles, books or a list of credits that an employer is going to want to know, prepare a traditional resume and then attach the list of credits or accomplishments.

Content

Appearance is important, but content is still the most important part of a resume. Great content that focuses on the employer's needs will get the most attention.

The next chapter, **Take Inventory**, helps you identify the skills you have to sell. Take the time to prepare a good inventory, because your inventory is the foundation of a great resume.

Don't create your inventory as you write your resume. Identify your skills, weaknesses and experience without thinking about the resume. List what you've done, your accomplishments and tasks independently. You won't include all of this information in your resume, but after doing the inventory, you'll better understand what you're selling and have an idea of what to include. Consider your inventory as the research for your resume.

You'll use two different kinds of resumes. The first is your *marketing* or *model* resume. The second is an *employer-specific* or *tailored* resume. Both are important and both need to be perfect. Everything in your resumes should help the employer quickly identify you as a candidate that should be talked to.

Don't waste an employer's time with redundant or obvious information. Show how you can resolve their problems, how you will add to their success and why you should be interviewed.

TAKE INVENTORY

Taking inventory is evaluating what you've done, what you know, how you add value, the problems you've solved and what you can do.

It's figuring out what you're selling—it's your product research.

One of the first rules of sales is to know the product. To make a sale you have to be able to explain how a product works, understand who wants or needs the product and its value in the market. That's what taking inventory is about. Job-hunting is the process of making a sale and to make the best sale you need to know your product inside and out.

An inventory helps you develop a strategy, create marketing materials and prepare for interviews. It's a step that's often neglected. Taking inventory can be hard, because it requires the kind of self-inspection that people hate doing. But if it's done right, it gives you a huge advantage in selling yourself.

For most people professional self-inspection consists of adding their last job description to an old resume to create a current resume. Resumes usually consist of a list of places and dates they've worked, short descriptions of daily tasks, a list of their most memorable accomplishments, education, designations and awards. And that's it.

An in-depth inventory consists of much more. It starts with your resume, but requires you to flesh it out, fill it in and summarize what you have done and who you've become in the process. Your inventory is *not* a resume. It's the foundation of your job search, but you won't send it out. The information in it becomes the building blocks for your resumes, your marketing material and your interviews.

First, start with the information in your resume: education, employment and experience. Next, add all of your other experiences and interests that define who you are and what you've done, like community organizations or involvement in a club or church. If you've been a homemaker, include it as one of your experiences. Go back as far as you can remember.

Next, break your timeline and accomplishments into three month blocks. What did you do in each of those blocks? What did you accomplish? How did you add value? List every accomplishment you can reasonably take credit for, include anything for which you were recognized or rewarded. Rack your brain and err on the side of taking credit—remember this list isn't for general consumption. It's a tool for your use. Be specific. Don't just write that you "increased sales." How *much* did you increase sales, how much responsibility did you handle, what were your accountabilities, what did you learn and what did you mess up?

Don't list the things you did only in the last couple of years; go back to the beginning. List *all* of your experiences so you can discover all of the skills you've developed over your career. You may find it useful to use old journals, calendars and those files of materials you've collected. These materials can help jog your memory and flesh out what you've been doing over your career.

Now, look at your accomplishments and list the skills you've developed. Skills are different from experience. Hopefully as you review the things you've accomplished you'll begin to see patterns of the skills and expertise you've developed; abilities your employers and friends have come to rely on and that will form the basis of your job search and marketing materials.

All of these lists—experiences, accomplishments and skills—define the product that you have to sell . . . You.

A list of past employers is important, but you won't be hired because of who you worked for. A successful job search results from articulating what you can do—the problems you can solve, the value you add and the transferable skills you bring to a new employer.

Sometimes skills are more transferable than you might think. If you're an expert using a specific computer application, you need to find out what other companies use that program. You may discover that you have a skill that is transferrable to organizations you never would have thought of approaching.

General skills can be harder to define. For example, you may have developed negotiation skills from working with your customers. Negotiation is a great skill to sell, but your personal experience may not help you in unrelated fields, because negotiation is usually a function of specialized knowledge about an industry or specific situations. For example, car salesmen are usually good negotiators but their knowledge of their customers and auto values might not translate well to the area of negotiating commercial property transactions. When you define a skill, think about how you developed it and the specific situations and knowledge someone would need to do what you've done.

Be realistic about your skills and abilities, but don't sell yourself short. Your skills are valuable and make you hirable. If you can solve actual problems for an employer and can give examples, include these skills on your inventory. For ideas and help in your self-inventory see **Appendix 2**.

The great thing about selling yourself, and understanding what you have to sell, is that you can continue to work on making your product better while you're trying to make a sale. In fact, you can sell the skills you're learning in your job search—discipline, creating strategies, sales and project management. Take inventory and you'll realize that you can take control, make a difference and make a sale.

Adding Value

To get a job, you only have to convince one employer that you can help them be successful. Employers are looking for solutions, for pieces of a puzzle, or a team member to help their companies achieve objectives. Companies don't hire people to fill seats because they have empty desks.

In a tough economy every position has to be justified; managers have to show that there's a need to be filled. If you are going to be the person who gets the job, you have to convince the employer—and specifically the decision-makers —that you're the one to solve *their* problems.

Employers look for good employees, hoping they can find a great one. A great employee meets job requirements, solves problems and adds value to the organization without serious flaws. You can simplify an employer's search by demonstrating that you do all of those things.

You can demonstrate that you add value in two ways. First, make it easy to find, interview and hire you. Second, focus on solving their problems—not your need to get a job.

Make It Easy for an Employer to Hire You

When you apply for a position or contact a potential employer you have to make it easy for them to find you, like you and see you as part of their organization. They need a reason to hire you and you can give it to them from the start.

Making it easy begins with focusing your strategy on potential employers. It starts with matching your resume to their needs and continues through the interview process as you demonstrate your desire to help them succeed.

A great resume is written for the employer who gets it. A company's website can teach you a lot about a company culture and mission. Job posts list requirements, responsibilities and the company's wish list of characteristics for a great candidate; and it's your guide for both what you say and for how you say it. Too many resumes and cover letters focus on what applicants want to say, usually using a "one size fits all" approach that's too focused on the applicant. Follow the employer's description, using the same words and style when preparing your cover letter and resume and you'll make it easier for the screeners to find your qualifications.

Follow an employer's instructions for submitting resumes, especially if they make specific formatting requests. Find out how an employer will use your resume. If you want to send extra material, make sure the employer wants to see it.

Make sure your resume looks clean and professional. When I was hiring people I got everything: normal resumes, short books, computer disks, e-mails, brochures, and websites. I received resumes on pink paper, color-printed with pictures, scented resumes and even one with the paper cut into odd shapes. Some were professionally produced, but many were poorly written and edited. The resumes that got my attention did so by clearly matching experience and talents to what I was looking for.

If you want to add some zing to your resume, take a look at the company's marketing materials and emulate (don't plagiarize) the feel and colors of their marketing materials. Employers are all different, so not every resume is going to work with every decision-maker. Try to make it easy for employers to discover your potential.

Create a resume that shows you understand the employer's problems and that you are focused on solving them. Follow instructions. Make sure everything you submit is professional, edited and geared toward that employer. Don't make it difficult to find your strengths and qualifications. Do everything you can to make it easy for the decision-makers to come up with reasons to interview you—and potentially to hire you.

Demonstrate How You Solve Problems

Companies have to make a return—a profit—on money they spend. If the owners or stockholders don't get a return on their investment, they will invest someplace else. You need to present your value in terms of the return on their investment. A company pays an employee and provides benefits—this is their investment. You need to show why it's a good investment to pay *you*.

Too many job hunters think that the application and interview process is about them. Wrong. Being a candidate is not about you—it's about the employer and how you will solve their problems. Always define your experience, education and character in a way that demonstrates how you solve problems, make money and improve a company—how you add value!

Even statements about your weaknesses or lack of qualifications should be answered in ways that demonstrate recognition and solutions. Sometimes in an application, or in an interview, you'll be asked about your weaknesses. It's not believable to say that your biggest weakness is that you work too hard. You know this question is going to be asked, be prepared with a good answer. This is a great way to add value and look competent.

So how do you answer a question about your weaknesses? From your inventory pick a weakness that you've worked on improving and then explain what you've done. Here's an example:

"My last employer thought that my writing skills were weak, so I took two classes on business writing. I'm still working on it, but I've really improved my ability to represent you in a professional and concise way."

This answer has all the elements you need to communicate: the weakness: the answer to the question, the solution and the value you bring to your next employer.

Your resume shouldn't be a laundry list of what you've done. It should provide concise explanations and stories about your impact. If you were an office manager, don't give a list of day-to-day activities (made coffee, filed papers, made more coffee). Instead, talk about how you made the business successful. Be specific about specific events, accomplishments and people and you'll be more compelling and memorable. You solved problems, organized, made work easier for everyone there, helped clients and had a direct impact on the profitability of the business. *This* is your value. *This* is what you are selling. Employers are not concerned about coffee-making skills.

Show your value by focusing your message on how you will make them money or save them money. How will you make them a more profitable, more successful and better company? If you can demonstrate exceptional value, you will find opportunities everywhere. Companies that aren't even looking for an employee can justify hiring you if you can make them more profitable!

Start thinking about yourself and your skills from the perspective of your impact, your value and why an employer would be crazy to pass up the opportunity to hire you today.

BIG COMPANY VS. SMALL COMPANY

There are differences in how you approach a big company versus your approach to smaller company. You need to understand these differences and the impact they'll have on your resume and strategy.

Big Companies

Big companies have more positions posted, but more barriers to applying for those positions. When I talk about big companies I'm thinking of companies with hundreds or thousands of employees in multiple locations. These companies have large HR and legal departments. They have sophisticated on-line job systems and these systems are administered by specialists who screen resumes and often prepare the posts you see.

There are a couple of things to know to successfully approach a big company. First, many positions are filled before they're posted. When I've worked for big companies I rarely posted a job where we didn't already have an internal candidate or outside candidates I was encouraging to apply for the position. Even if I knew who was going to fill a position I still had to post it. I also had to interview most of the qualified internal candidates and several outside candidates. Large companies develop these policies to protect themselves.

Second, the initial screeners usually don't know anything about the positions being filled. They prepare the posts using buzzwords from position descriptions and then look for the buzzwords in the resumes they receive. Their job is to take a hundred applications and get it down to ten or fifteen—and some hiring managers only ask for three or four.

Third, the system is set up to keep the applicant from ever talking to a real person unless they want to talk to you. The larger the company the harder it is to find a decision-maker or person responsible for a specific position. Big companies are full of bureaucracy. You just have to figure out how to get around it if you can and work through it if you can't.

One of my most amazing experiences with a big company was when I was called by a professional friend and asked if I'd be interested in joining his division. I was interested in the opportunity so he asked me to send my resume, which I did. He called a couple of days later to let me know that he was going to have to put the position into their on-line system and I would have to apply through the system—but he assured me that I was only candidate they wanted. They used my resume to create the job post . . . I have never been more qualified for a specific position!

I submitted my resume and waited for the next step, an interview with senior management. Imagine my surprise when I received a letter letting me know that I wasn't qualified for the job; but they were going to keep my resume for a year in case something else came up. I immediately called my friend who just laughed. They had received over fifty applications for the job, and despite the fact that I was the "perfect" match I was screened out by HR. I got the job and I kept the letter.

My experience illustrates some of the problems with big companies and the defenses they build to protect themselves. The job was mine, but two other outside candidates were brought in so boxes could be checked. Even though I was the most qualified candidate I didn't get through the initial screening. I was never able to find out who sent the letter, but I worked with HR while I was with that company and I came to understand the limitations and problems they faced. Sometimes a screener gets enough resumes that meet the basic qualifications and they quit looking.

Here's what I've learned about approaching big companies:

- You significantly improve your chances of getting an interview if you can get through to a decision-maker. Find out who the decision-makers are; use your network, make calls and do some research. Get the attention of a decision-maker and send a resume directly to them.
- When you use an on-line application system use the language of the job description in your resume; give them what they're asking for. See the chapter on **The On-Line Resume**.
- Try to get the name and contact information of an internal recruiter. Once you have a name, you know someone you can

contact for more information about new posts. I've successfully used internal recruiters to get initial interviews for several posts at the same company.
- With a big company you really have to take the hiring process one step at a time. You have to create a resume that follows the post to get past the screeners. You have to say the right things during the screening interviews and work purposefully to get to the final interview rounds.
- You have to be patient. Large companies take forever. Resumes are reviewed by committees. They get passed around and decisions on who to interview and who progresses at each round take time.
- Be ultra-professional. Screeners are looking for errors as a way to eliminate resumes and candidates. Proofread your resumes and communications several times and use your editors before they go out.
- Apply down—by this I mean you need to consider applying for positions that you're over-qualified for. Decision-makers at bigger companies often look down on experience at smaller companies. Sometimes you need to take a lesser role to get a foot in the door and to get the position you really want.

Small Companies

Small companies are different because they don't have as many barriers to getting to the decision-makers and they often don't have a lot of process in place. Depending on the size and structure of the company the HR department may also be the president or owner of the company. I've found that it's much easier to get interviews with small companies, but it's less predictable how and when they'll make a final decision.

I've had some of my most interesting experiences with smaller companies. I was offered a position over the phone without having an in-person interview; and I was really concerned about why they'd offer me a job without meeting me! For another position I spent a day in an office meeting over a dozen people including the president and the senior managers and they asked me one question that I answered the whole day! All they did was tell me about what they were doing.

Small companies don't have lawyers reviewing interview questions. I've been asked questions that were illegal and I had one manager tell me he knew the question was illegal, but he needed to know the answer before he'd think about hiring me.

You have to be flexible, positions are not always well defined and titles can be deceiving. Small companies are sometimes willing to let you use any title you want if you'll take less money.

Just because there are fewer barriers to getting to the decision-makers doesn't mean it's easier. When a company only has a few employees the right fit is essential. Hiring the wrong person can have a huge impact on the survival of a small company. Everything you do, every interaction, is important. Here are some ways to get noticed and maximize your chances of being hired.

- If you're coming from a big company make sure you emphasize the variety of skills and experience you have. Small companies have their own biases against big employers and one perception is that employees of big companies are button pushers; that tasks and positions are so specialized that you won't be able to adapt to less structure and more demands.
- Use your resume and cover letter to communicate your willingness to do what needs to be done. I once went from a company where I wasn't allowed to move my computer (that was IT's job) to a company where I helped clean the kitchen and emptied my own garbage. Small companies have to be lean and nothing eliminates a candidate faster than a sense of entitlement or needing lots of support.
- Research the company's products, mission, people and history. Read everything on the website. Pull financials and look for current and old news. Knowing that Thomas Edison founded GE won't help much when you interview with one of their divisions, but knowing that the president's grandfather started the company that's interviewing you can be a big help.
- Simplify your resume. Smaller companies use fewer acronyms and buzz words. Job posts are usually more to the point and

your resume needs to get to the point as well. Shorten your resume and use every opportunity in your job and skill descriptions to demonstrate why you meet their qualifications. There probably won't be a HR hiring specialist filtering resumes in a smaller company, it'll be the decision-maker looking at resumes trying to decide who to talk to.

- Make it easy for the decision-maker to meet you. I've offered to meet with an employer at a small company at my expense when the company was within driving distance. One time I was going to a city for a family trip and I contacted a company owner and asked for 30 minutes to introduce myself. With small companies you can even go door to door asking to meet the manager or owner.

To be a successful job-hunter you have to convince decision-makers that if you're hired you'll make the company better. Understanding the differences between big companies and small companies can make a difference in how effective you are in getting to decision-makers and overcoming their objections and concerns.

FORMAT AND FIRST IMPRESSIONS

Your resume's format is vital to the impression you make and image you create when someone looks at your resume for the first time. There's a reason that companies pay big money to design ads and marketing material—design and appearance matter.

On the other hand, a resume is a resume.

Your Resume Needs to be a Resume

Here's the problem. You want your resume to stick out and to be noticed. But you don't want it to stick out so much that the first impression is to reject it!

Most employers still want resumes. They want resumes that look like resumes. They compare resumes to other resumes, both the presentation and the content. They want to be able to find information quickly, and it helps them when you use formats that are familiar and easy to navigate.

I've received resumes that were printed on bright colored paper, resumes where the text was printed at weird angles, resumes with the paper cut into strange shapes and resumes with creative, but confusing, graphic designs dominating the page. I've received resumes in the form of short stories, one that was a long and hard to read poem, one designed to look like a photo album and several that were scented. I didn't interview any of these candidates.

Being too creative with a resume is usually just distracting. I wasn't looking to fill creative positions. These resumes might have been effective for design positions—or in-house poets—but for most companies and most positions a resume should look like a resume to be effective.

So how do you make your resume more effective? How do you stand out when an employer is going to receive hundreds of resumes? The simple answer is to make it as perfect as you can for that employer and the needs they're trying to fill.

Your Resume's Format

There are lots of sample resumes on the internet. There are books about how to format and organize resumes. Many of them claim to have the best look or organization, but since employers aren't reading these books they usually don't know what's trendy or supposed to work best on any given day.

I'm writing this in Word right now and I just checked resume templates—there are over sixty templates for resumes in my version of Word. And all of them look great.

I'm not including examples of resumes because there are so many different ones that are available, and because I know from experience that no design is going to work for every decision-maker, but here are some things for you to consider regarding your resume's format:

- Be consistent. When you use formatting for headings and sections, don't change formatting in the middle of the resume. Create a style guide or simple rules for formatting and use them consistently.
- Don't use lots of fonts and special effects. Your resume should be all in the same font or no more than two fonts that complement each other. There are publication design guides that can give you information on fonts and which ones work together.
- Don't use a lot of different font sizes. Be consistent and don't use fonts that are too small, or too big. For most business fonts (which you should be using) your font size should be between 11 and 14 for the headings, subheadings and paragraphs.
- Don't leave huge white spaces. I've seen resumes with big empty spaces between sections or to the right of the text. If you really don't have that much to communicate put everything on one page; better yet, go back and finish your personal inventory so you have more material to include—the skills and experience an employer needs.
- Avoid photos in your resume. I've only seen a couple of resumes where it worked. Usually, photos in resumes are too

small. They don't scan well. Unless the interview is an audition, photos of yourself won't help you get an interview.

Resume Sections

Most resumes have the same sections. Which sections you include depends on what the employer is looking for. Here are the mandatory sections:

Identification: Your resume needs to have your name and contact information prominently displayed. I have my name in large, bold letters at the top of each page, with my address, phone and email on the first page. Make it easy for employers to know how to contact you.

Summary/Objectives/Skill List: These sections usually start your resume, so make your introduction stand out. Tell the decision-maker who you are and what you can do for them from the start. If this section doesn't get their attention they may not read the rest of the resume.

I like Summary sections, especially if they help me know what the resume says and I can easily understand how you meet my needs. Because I prefer Summaries I focus more on how to create a good one in this book. See the next chapter for more detail on creating a Summary section.

I don't like Objective sections; because an Objectives section tell me things I already know as an employer. I know you're looking for a job and I suspect you'd like the job you applied for.

Skill Lists, a list of what you think you're good at, are increasingly popular as an introductory section. Skill Lists can help HR screeners or resume software find specific words or phrases—but they're easy to skip over and not attention grabbing.

Education: You have to include an education section. This is mandatory. Include accomplishments and extra-curricular activities if they're recent or pertinent to the employer.

Employment/Experience: This is the big section; where most decision-makers go right away. There are several ways you can organize this section, but the goal is to show your ability to help a potential employer. This is not a self-aggrandizing exercise; remember—your resume is not really about you. You need to show how you meet an employer's requirements and will help them make money or solve a problem. Your Summary section claims you can do this, and your Experience section shows how you've done it in the past and illuminates your skills.

There are other sections you can use in a resume, but they aren't mandatory and you use them to help your reader—not to feed your ego or make your resume longer. Some of these sections include:

Accomplishments/Awards: Include accomplishments that help you demonstrate your value. These are things you do or have done that don't fit into your employment history. For new professionals this can include academic accomplishments, contests and extracurricular activities.

Publications/Presentations. You can also include sections for publications or presentations. These sections are common for academic CV's where professors have long lists of articles, books or book contributions, and professional presentations that are important for their career development. Include enough information to allow an employer to find published material.

Projects: I've been involved in and led many special projects and I like to let employers see both how many and the nature of these projects. I don't include a lot of information, usually just a list. In my Experience section I identify where the projects were done. Here's an example of my Project Management section:

> **Project Management:** Due Diligence and Strategy • Best Practice Implementation • IT Design and Implementation • Vendor Management • Process Audits • Training • New Employee Hiring and Orientation • Fiscal Evaluation Procedures and Adequacy • Guidelines and Measurement • Interdepartmental Communication and Coordination • Trends and Opportunities Task Force

This is different than my summary section and focuses on one of the skill sets that sets me apart and helps me add value. Each project is also a story I can tell in an interview if asked.

Community/Professional Involvement: This is an optional section for accomplishments that aren't professional but come from your involvement in recognized organizations or community roles. If you've been on a school board, president of a community organization or deeply involved in a national organization, here's where you can list these accomplishments. Be careful about including activities that an employer will be concerned will interfere with your work. It's great to list your service on a school board; however, being the national leader of a controversial political organization is going to set off alarms.

Interests/Hobbies: If you've been in the workplace for more than a couple of years don't include an Interests section. This is resume filler when you don't have work experience.

One thing to remember about your resume sections is that they don't have to be in the same order for every employer or job post. Always lead with the sections that help you the most. If you have an advanced degree and they want an advanced degree, put education towards the front. If you don't have an advanced degree, lead with your relevant experience and accomplishments and move education back.

Organization – Chronological or Functional

There are two primary ways to organize your Experience section: by employer in chronological order, or by function or skill set. I am heavily biased towards chronological and here's why.

First, it's the most common and what screeners and decision-makers are used to seeing. If your resume is hard to compare to other resumes it can be screened out just for being different.

Second, when I look at a resume I want to know who you worked for, what your title was and what you did at that company. If I have to look at your skills section and then try to match it to your list of employers (which you still should include) it's just too much work when I have many more resumes to look at.

Third, a functional or skills section is harder to write well. Most of the functional sections I've reviewed were much harder to read and understand; if you led a project I really want to know when it was in your career, for whom and in what role. I have a list of projects I've managed in my resume, but the projects themselves are described in the Employment section, in chronological order.

Fourth, functional resumes are harder to translate to on-line application systems. Most application software systems use chronological input of employment and experience.

Fifth, and last, when I see a functional resume I suspect that the candidate is trying to hide something. It could be that the only time they did the job I'm looking to fill was for their first employer ten years ago! It might be to hide a break in employment or to hide a career track that wasn't traditional. Even if it's not true, a functional resume is harder to create and read because it's harder to organize your experience and accomplishments in context without being redundant.

There are experts who will vigorously disagree with me. They, and you, are entitled to have a different opinion. There are lots of good materials and books available on-line or in your library on formatting your resume and building chronological and functional resumes.

Remember that your goal is to make it easy for a potential employer to identify you as a candidate they want to interview. So make it easy to find the skills, education and experience they need.

The Look

How a resume looks is important. Not as important as what it says, but a resume that's poorly designed may not be read at all. When you finish your resume pin it on the wall. Back up and look at it. Does it look good? Are the sections evenly distributed? Are sections broken up by page breaks or design elements?

Make sure that section and subsection headings are consistent, using the same fonts and font sizes. If you use a header section make sure it looks the same on all pages. Include page numbers on your resume, I like to tell readers what page they're on and how many pages there are . . . "Page 1 of 2".

If you use a template and don't change the formatting you shouldn't have problems, but you should circulate your resume to your advisory group and get opinions on both content and style.

Resume Grammar

Resume grammar is unique in that the normal rules of sentence structure don't apply. For example, don't use the word "I" to start every sentence. The reader knows the resume is about you, so you shouldn't include a proper subject. It's also distracting when every sentence starts with the same words. For example:

"I led a critical IT project" becomes "Led a critical IT project".

"I exceeded sales objectives by 25%" becomes "Exceeded sales objectives by 25%".

Make sure that you don't use the same power words to start every sentence or description. I've seen resumes where the candidate "Led" everything. Find other words to use, such as managed, ran, organized or directed. Think of other words that have similar but more powerful impressions; did you lead or did you build. Were you a manager or an executive?

Make sure that you use the right word. It's amazing how many professionals with years of college forget that spell check can't tell whether you should use "too" or "to"; "there", "their" or "they're"; or "where", "were" or "wear".

Make sure you have subject and verb agreement. Resume writers sometimes forget who the subject of the sentence is, especially if the subject, "I", isn't in the sentence.

Use punctuation appropriately. Know when to use semi-colons; and when to use colons. Don't over-use comas. Keep sentences short and easy to read.

Make your resume as perfect as you can.

Making it Perfect

You can't control what happens with your resume when an employer receives it. You don't know who will look at it and why they may reject it, or if they'll decide to call you for an interview. What you can control is how it's written before you send it out.

Make it easy to use. Your resume is a sales brochure with the objective of convincing a potential employer to interview you. It should be about what that employer needs and is looking for. Your Summary should introduce the information in the rest of the resume and convince the reader to keep going. Your sections should be written to demonstrate the skills and experience the employer needs. You can and should toot your own horn, but never forget to stay focused on the employer.

Don't make stupid mistakes. I can't tell you that I've never had a spelling error in my resume. But when I find them after I've sent my resume I don't hold my breath for an interview. Your resume is the first work-product a potential employer will see. When they're trying to eliminate resumes from the "need to talk to" stack, spelling and obvious grammar errors are as good a reason as any to eliminate you.

The first impression you'll get to make is with your resume. Take the time to get it right.

The Model Resume

Your model resume is the resume you create for your dream job—for the employer and position you'd like to find. A model resume should be perfect, if only because you have time to work on it and make it perfect. It should focus on your strengths. It should be the best marketing brochure you can create. It will be the foundation of the resumes you prepare for specific employers and for specific positions.

Your model resume is what you hand out at networking events, or give to someone who's not looking to fill a specific position. As you develop your model resume, design each section separately. The components can be changed around and organized differently depending on your audience and purpose.

Objectives / Summaries / Skill Lists

Many resumes start with a statement of objectives, a summary and/or a list of skills as an introduction. While this is the first thing on the resume, it's the last section you should create. Start with your employment section, education and other accomplishments, then go back and summarize the really big points you want the reader to notice. The Summary should be like a table of contents that helps the reader know what's coming—and you don't start a book by writing the table of contents.

Objectives: The typical "Objectives" section is a waste of space and the reader's time, because most applicants put obvious, self-centered information in their objectives (I admit I'm biased). Here's what I've seen in a typical objective section:

Sales professional seeking a challenging sales management position.

Or:

Retail sales professional looking for a sales or entry-level management position where I use my talents and skills for customer service.

These objectives are about what *you* want. As an employer, I'm already pretty sure what you want—you sent me a resume.

What you need is a section that's focused on what matters to me, the employer.

Summary: A summary section is a narrative introduction to your resume. This summary was written from information in the resume and is designed for the writer's perfect job:

> Sales professional with over six years of experience in relationship development and high-profile, high-impact sales. Exceeded sales objectives every year, contributing to company profitability. Expert in CRM software and training. Focused on customer service, problem-solving and building profitable sales relationships. Disciplined work that produced superior sales results.

This summary states the value this applicant has to offer and tells me what I'm going to find in this resume.

Skills List. It's become popular to include a list of your skills or core strengths at the beginning of a resume. I don't like lists of skills or strengths and rarely read them, but other decision-makers may and there are reasons to include a list.

A skills list can help if you know that the resume will be screened by HR or a software system. A skill list (with the right skills, of course) makes it easy to find key words. Resume software can eliminate resumes that don't have specific words; but the key words don't have to be in a specific section. They can be in a list, a summary or in the text of the resume.

I prefer to use a strong, narrative summary as a way to introduce the rest of the resume, and it can be very effective if it reflects the requirements and language an employer used to describe the job.

Whether you use a summary section or skill list, make sure the rest of the resume supports your claims. One of the most common mistakes people make is to list strengths like time management or communication and then fail to support those skills in the rest of the resume. One of my favorite reasons to reject a resume was to have someone claim to be detail oriented and then have a resume full of spelling, punctuation and formatting errors.

Contact Information

Make sure contact information is easy to find. It can be part of the header or a separate category in the body of the resume. Make sure when transferring your resume to a database you don't leave contact information out because it's in your document header.

Include phone numbers that work. If you have voice mail or an answering machine, use an appropriate voice message. Make sure your contact information works and helps you appear professional.

Education/Professional Designations

Whether you lead with education or employment depends on what's more important for your dream job. If your dream job requires specific education or licenses, or if you think your education or designations give you a competitive advantage, put your education first so employers don't have to search for it. Whatever you lead with is the most likely to seen before your resume is rejected, so lead with your strongest message or qualifications.

Include degrees, institutions and location of the schools. Include licenses and professional designations. You can also include professional courses you've taken and certificates you've received. These aren't official degrees, but they demonstrate a commitment to continuing improvement—a skill you can sell.

Employment/Work Experience

This is the big section, the one that employers expect to see—the positions you've held and the titles you've been given. Employers look at titles and try to match your job titles to what they're looking for. I include the general location of past employers, like Denver, Colorado, but not addresses or supervisor names.

Describe your responsibilities and accomplishments in a way that emphasizes your value to each organization you've worked for—and the skills you're bringing to a new employer. Try to match the descriptions of your past responsibilities to the duties of your target job. Look at examples of job postings for the kind of job you're targeting (whether you're applying for them or not) and use those descriptions to flesh out the responsibilities you've had and the contributions you've made.

Whether you use a summary or a skills list, make sure that your employment section supports your introduction. If you put down that you have presentation or management experience, the job history must support these claims. If you find you can't support what you put into your summary or list, go back and change it.

Here's an employment description from a hypothetical resume:

Marketing Sales Director
ACME Product Company, Indianapolis, IN   2001–2008
Led a team of ten associates in developing and marketing new product lines. Designed customer-feedback survey. Coordinated marketing and sales and managed development of new products for region. Responsible for successful new product launches. Responsible for operations, hiring and training.

But this is better:

Marketing Sales Director
ACME Product Company , Indianapolis, IN   2001–2008
Led ten-member team responsible for regional marketing, sales, and national development and launch of new products. Managed customer-service initiative, including design of customer-feedback survey. Regional accountability for over $22 million in annual sales, exceeding profitability objectives and new product launches. Responsible for over $5 million in annual revenue. Exceeded position objectives for revenue, profitability, operations, training, and employee mentoring and development.

Don't make things up. Use actual numbers if you can remember or recreate them. Don't just say that sales went up. Talk about specific measurements: "responsible for 23% increase in sales over 16-month period."

Another approach is to use bullet points to articulate each point that you want to make.

Marketing Sales Director
ACME Product Company, Indianapolis, IN   2001–2008
- Lead ten-member regional marketing and sales team; responsible for over $22 million in annual sales.
- Over 18% average annual increase in revenue from 2002 to year-end 2007.
- Exceeded sales and profitability objectives for 2004 to 2007.
- Responsible for development and launch of new products nationally, resulting in over $5 million in annual revenue.
- Managed customer-service initiative; including design of customer-feedback survey.
- Exceeded position objectives for revenue, department profitability, operations, training, and employee mentoring and development.

Whether you're an assistant or an executive, your resume should focus on your experience and your value. Include titles, how you improved the company, how you dealt with employees and helped customers. Focus on the skills you're selling.

The same applies if you want to jump to another career field. If you've been in sales but want to try management, or you're a professional wanting to move to a more traditional management position, emphasize transferable skills. Don't use specific accomplishments if they don't show how you can create value for a different industry. Focus on results, skills and abilities that transfer well. Don't get hung up on your former titles or use jargon from your previous field that will have little meaning to an employer in a different industry.

Personal Accomplishments & Interests

Personal accomplishments are what you want to tell potential employers that don't fit anywhere else. For example, you can use a catchall section, titled "Personal Interests," to include the fact that you are a champion ballroom dancer, bowler or like to bicycle.

You can also include special sections for specific type of accomplishments. I've written on professional topics, so in my resume I include a list of the articles and book chapters I've written.

The question is whether you *should* include these interests and accomplishments? The short answer is to include only the information that helps display your skills and value for an employer. If your resume is light on employment history it can help to include activities that demonstrate these abilities.

Include your involvement, especially responsibilities and leadership, in organizations and community groups. But don't scare away potential employers with activities that might compete with your commitment to their company. Include anything that's related to job skills, specifically skills or experiences like performing or speaking. On occasion I include speaking competitions I've been in if I want to focus on my communication skills. If your outside experiences are the basis for skills you're offering to an employer, then include them.

Include activities that can set you apart and may lead to interview questions that let you showcase your unique qualities.

Don't exaggerate your accomplishments. And don't lie. Everything on your resume is fair game for questions and background checks during the interview process.

The Finished Product

Your finished model resume should be as perfect as you can make it. This is your primary work product that decision-makers will review and from it they'll form opinions about you. Make sure there's no spelling mistakes, glaring grammar problems and that it looks good and is consistent in tone and structure.

Have other people review it. Use your friends and family who are good at editing. Contact work friends and former employers and ask them to look at it and make suggestions. Edit it over and over. Read it out loud, read it backwards. Change the sections around and use different templates until you get the look you want.

It's important that you create your resume yourself. I know there are services that can put together great looking resumes for you. But I believe that that it's essential for you to go through the effort of creating a great resume.

I've had candidates in interviews who hadn't written their own resumes. I could tell because they couldn't find information or weren't familiar with the terms and descriptions. In an interview I asked a candidate what he meant by "leveraging" his resources—a phrase he used several times in his resume. He didn't know, which meant he either took the phrase from an article or someone else's resume . . . or someone else had written his resume. You look bad when you don't know what's in your own resume, or don't know the meaning of phrases or acronyms.

Take the time to create a great model resume. It gives you a model for tailored resumes, it's a document you can hand out, and the time you spend preparing a great resume will help you prepare for the interviews a perfect resume will get you.

The Tailored Resume

When you have your model resume edited and perfected, you have the starting point for modifying your resume to submit for specific jobs. There are two situations where you wouldn't use a tailored resume: when you don't have a job description or when the job you're applying for is your dream position—the one you prepared your resume for. Otherwise, change your resume. You want to make it as easy as possible for an employer to match your background and experience to their specific requirements.

Before you make any changes in your resume, research the company to get a sense of what they do, how they're organized, and who they are. Read the job description carefully—what are they looking for? Are they stressing specific education or background? What skills do they need? What problems need to solved? Once you've figured out the answers to these questions, change your resume to show how you meet their needs.

Here's an example of a management job description that requires specific experience and education.

Manager, Business Development

Reporting to the division president, the Manager of Business Development will be given the task to achieve growth & profit goals of business group(s) and optimize technical resources through the development and execution of marketing plans for the Division. Specific duties include:

—Develop and implement market-driven business plans, strategies, and tactics for business group to ensure business income objectives are met

—Identify key industry opportunities and develop thrust plans

—Develop product plans for new development and product improvement working with representative feedback, competitive analysis, and customer input

—Provide operating forecast for business group

—Position price and cost of products

—Provide promotion and documentation for all industry groups within business group

—Assume full industry planning and project-management responsibility for pipeline and new development markets

Requirements
—Four-year bachelor's degree required, with MBA in Marketing or Finance preferred.
—Experience in sales, marketing or business development a plus
—Polished relationship-management skills to prospect and uncover new opportunities
—Strong leadership skills, program management and pursuit/capture experience
—Proposal-preparation skills, and excellent customer-interface skills
—Ability to manage multiple and/or changing priorities
—Demonstrated professional expertise with clear understanding of the company's business, processes and procedures.

This is a typical job post, a wish list that describes the perfect candidate, an internal candidate or the person who just left! As a candidate, you have to identify the skills they're looking for—and create a resume that makes it easy for them to see how you meet their needs.

So what skills and experience should an applicant focus on for this position? Take the job description apart, identify the criteria that are important to the decision-maker and modify your resume to persuade them that they need to talk to you.

What is this potential employer looking for? What's really important to them and what skills will get you noticed?

Manager, Business Development
Reporting to the division president, the Manager of Business Development will be given the task to **achieve growth & profit goals** *of business group(s) and optimize technical resources through the development and execution of marketing plans for the Division.*

The theme throughout this description is growth and profit. This employer isn't going to hire someone who can just "optimize technical resources"; they want someone who knows how to grow profitable business. If you're going to get an interview you're going to have to persuade them of your ability to make money for them.

Now look for the key words, the terms that they use to describe the functions and skills of a successful candidate.

> *Specific duties include:*
> *—**develop and implement** market-driven business plans, **strategies**, and tactics for business group **to ensure business income objectives are met***

Don't get bogged down in the overuse of buzz words—get to the heart of the matter and you'll find the skills the employer wants to see that you have!

> *—identify **key industry opportunities** and **develop thrust plans***

Know what a thrust plan is . . . as an applicant I would focus on my knowledge of industry opportunities, specifically the people I know and can contact on behalf of this employer.

> *—develop product plans for **new development** and **product improvement** working with representative feedback, competitive analysis, and customer input*

It's not clear whether they want to develop new products, or just new markets for the products they have (and want to improve). Cover both and demonstrate your ability to develop new markets, new products and your obsession with improving the products you sell.

> *—provide operating **forecast** for business group*
> *—position price and cost of products*
> *—provide **promotion** and documentation for all industry groups within business group*
> *—assume full industry **planning** and **project-management** responsibility for pipeline and new development markets*

These are key words you want to include in your resume. Don't gloss over these duties, they may be important to individual decision-makers, but don't lose site of the real focus—this job is going to someone who proves they can produce profitable growth!

> *Requirements*
> *Qualifications:*
> *—Four-year **bachelor's degree required**, with **MBA** in Marketing or Finance preferred.*

You have to have the bachelor's degree and you'll probably be competing with MBAs. Make sure readers can find these qualifications quickly.

> —Experience in **sales, marketing or business development** a plus
> —polished **relationship-management** skills to prospect and uncover **new opportunities**
> —strong **leadership** skills, **program management** and **pursuit/capture** experience
> —**proposal-preparation** skills, and excellent **customer-interface skills**
> —ability to manage multiple and/or changing priorities

Here are more key words to use in your summary and employment history. None of these "requirements" are substantial in the sense that it can be objectively proved you have them. By telling them about your successes in leading product development and sales you'll show you have these qualities—use *these* words in your resume.

> —demonstrated professional expertise with **clear understanding of the company's business, processes and procedures**.

This requirement is problematic since outside candidates rarely have a "clear understanding" of an employer's processes and procedures. Focus on your ability to learn, and see what you can find out about the company from research and networking.

Remember, the goal of your resume is to get an interview. You're not going to get a job offer from your resume. Match your resume to their needs; make it persuasive and easy to read. A resume is persuasive when it looks professional and demonstrates that you meet their needs.

So what changes do you make to create an employer-specific resume? You need to change everything that applies to this specific employer's needs. You'll need to modify qualifications, take out irrelevant experiences and add key words to match the job description.

If you have a summary section, customize it. Here is an example of a summary from a general resume, before it's modified to apply for this Business Manager position.

> **SUMMARY**
> Sales and marketing management professional with over ten years of developing profitable sales strategies and building client relationships. Exceeded sales targets and management objectives, resulting in profitable business development—annual sales growth over 12% (with industry average below 9%). Managed successful sales teams with emphasis on development, support, training and accountability. Experienced in new product sales strategy focusing on training, prospect development and internal systems.

It's a good summary. It's clear that the applicant has the experience the employer is looking for. But the potential employer has to search through the employment history to find the specific marketing characteristics they're looking for.

What you want is to make sure that your experience and ability is easy to find. I usually cut and paste the job description into my summary section and then edit to rewrite my summary.

> **SUMMARY**
> Management professional with success in achieving profitable growth in sales, marketing and business development. Relationship management skills. Prospect and new product development. Extensive industry knowledge and contacts. Leadership skills, program management and pursuit/capture experience. Professional proposals and presentations. Excellent customer interface skills, with a demonstrated ability to manage multiple and changing priorities internally and externally. Exceeded management objectives for gross sales, growth and profitability. Achieved 125% of industry average sales growth. Experienced in competitive analysis, feedback and utilization of customer input.

Notice how this summary emphasizes management experience and made it clear that the candidate knows the industry and has the contacts and experience to help the employer grow. Same applicant, same experience, but the job post provided the framework for how that experience is defined and emphasized—and the words that are used to describe it.

It also helps screeners find the key words they're looking for so there's more of a chance that the resume gets to decision-makers.

The employer wants someone who can help them be profitable (most employers are looking for this), so tell them about your experience in being responsible for, focused on and obsessed about increasing sales and making money for past employers. If you have the experience an employer is looking for, TELL THEM.

When you've finished your summary section, modify the rest of your resume to support it. Change employment descriptions to match the summary and align with the job description—review the organization of your resume to make sure that you're emphasizing your strengths.

The section following your summary should be the one that helps you the most. For example, the post says that a MBA is desired but not required; if you have a MBA put education before employment history—if you don't, move education to follow your experience and results.

Change your employment history to illustrate your experience and the specific results the employer is looking for. In this case you'd focus on developing strategies, building customer relationships, and increasing sales. Make it easy for this employer to see that you have relevant and valuable experience—and that you should be interviewed. Your employment history section has to support your summary. When you put facts, skills and numbers in the summary, make sure your claims are substantiated in your employment history.

Include other experiences or skills only if they demonstrate how you meet that employer's needs. Get rid of the fluff—anything that doesn't apply to this position. Before you send out a tailored resume, run it by your editors to make sure there are no errors. Print it and read it aloud, then read it backwards. Pin it on the wall and see how it looks. Demonstrate your professionalism through the quality of your work product.

The Online Resume

You often have to upload resumes to apply to online posting systems. Many job and professional sites allow you, and encourage you, to post a resume online. Here are some thoughts about your "online" resumes.

- For public websites be careful about the information you post or leave in a resume. If you're putting your resume on an open or searchable website take out identifying information that can be used by identity thieves.
- Be very general about employers, dates, locations, titles and your education. Use broad descriptions of accomplishments and responsibilities. There are two reasons for this: first, you don't want employers to assume things because of previous employers and job titles; and second, you don't want your tailored resume for a specific job to be compared to a general resume on a job site.
- Don't include identifying information on your resume if you don't have to. Use a generic email address with no names or identifiers. Be very broad identifying the geographic area you live in.
- Posted resumes should be short. Highlight your skills and briefly outline your work experience. No one reads resumes online; at best they skim them.
- Which brings me to an important observation—employers are generally not looking at on-line resumes for potential employees. There may be a few fields where employees can post a resume and expect legitimate inquiries from an employer, but most employers post openings and expect potential employees to apply.

Who looks at your online resume? People who want to sell you services or products – and scammers. When I've posted resumes the only response I've ever gotten were from resume drafting services, fee for service head-hunters, and dubious "employers" who promised great positions if I was willing to pay transaction fees.

You may have gotten the impression that I'm not a big fan of posting your resume online . . . and you'd be right. I've heard more stories about companies looking for the resumes of current employees than looking for resumes of potential employees. If your current employer finds your resume on a job site, it's usually not a career enhancing situation.

Online Applications

There's a big difference between posting your resume online and posting for a position through an online application program. Many posting programs allow or require you to upload a resume. The systems usually extract information from your resume and fill out the application forms—but they make serious mistakes extracting your information. The most important thing you have to do is carefully review the application information and make sure that it's correct. I find I always have to make changes to on-line applications because these systems have trouble identifying the employers on my resume.

The initial screening process usually uses data from the system generated application. Make sure that you spend time editing and reviewing your on-line application. The tendency is to get the information in as quickly as possible or rely on the auto-functions of the application process. This is still your work product and you'll be rejected for incoherent information or failing to look professional.

THE LEAP FROG RESUME

The leap frog resume is your resume for a position that's a stretch for your qualifications. It's skipping a level of management experience or taking on responsibilities that you believe you can handle, but haven't yet in your career. In the best of times jumping ahead is difficult, but it can be especially hard in a bad economy where there are so many qualified applicants.

It's more likely you'll be able to leap-frog into a new position with a current employer or because of an existing relationship—through your network. Applying for a stretch position with an employer who doesn't know you is difficult, but it doesn't mean you shouldn't try. Remember, let them say no—don't reject yourself before you apply.

It can be difficult to apply for positions that appear to be several levels above your last job, even if you've done the work and can handle the responsibility.

After a couple of years with my first employer, I was promoted to a supervisor position. A couple of months after starting the new position, the regional manager I reported to left for another company and I was asked to assume his responsibilities for a short time. That "short time" lasted 18 months and I became proficient at handling both supervisor and regional manager responsibilities. Because of my great performance, I was allowed to apply for the regional manager slot when home office got around to filling it. But I was passed over because they preferred to promote someone who had worked more years—as a supervisor!

I decided to look for another job rather than go back to being a supervisor who would have to train the new regional manager—but what I really wanted was a manager's job. I knew I could do it, and I was good at it. But how should I market myself?

Here are some suggestions, including a couple of tools that I used, that can help you.

- Use the title. I went to my boss and asked him what he thought my title should be while I was acting as a regional manager. He suggested that for resume purposes I was free to call myself a regional manager and that he'd support me if he was called for references. If your immediate manager or someone above you will support your use of a title—even if it was never official—then use it. But don't use a title if no one at a previous employer will support it.

- Use "Acting" title. I needed a resume for use within the company and didn't want to use a title that HR would object to. So I described my experience in two different paragraphs. One was labeled supervisor and described my accomplishments in that role, the second I labeled "Acting Regional Manager" and described those responsibilities and accomplishments.
- Don't use titles. Titles help potential employers immediately peg you as a candidate—but you have the option not to use them if the actual titles get in the way of being interviewed. Instead of labeling myself a "Supervisor," it would have been appropriate to use a description, "Regional operations/service manager." If you decide to drop titles, just make sure the description is accurate and the rest of your resume is consistent. This is also a good tool if you've been working someplace where titles were never updated, or they used unique titles.
- Most big career moves come from your network (people who know you) or a current employer who recognizes your ability. The challenge of moving several rungs up the ladder with a company that doesn't know you is that resumes are often eliminated when your experience doesn't compare with other candidates—no matter what title you use.
- Focus on your accomplishments. Be vague with the amount of time in the positions you've had. Your weakness is a lack of experience—so focus on what you've accomplished with the time you've had.
- Focus on leadership of projects, teams and special events. Describe examples of mentoring and client service that illustrate the characteristics the employer is looking for. Long before you get an interview, know how you're going to answer questions about your lack of experience, the stories you're going to tell and the examples you're going to give of the

accomplishments and skills you'd bring to the position. When you know how you're going to make your case, let your resume reflect your strategy. Create a strong cover letter that fleshes out your story and selling points.
- Start your resume and cover letter with your strongest arguments and most persuasive points. When an employer has candidates with the experience and titles they're looking for you will have to impress them quickly if you're going make it past the first screening process.

I didn't find a position comparable to the regional manager spot with a large employer, but I was able to use my experience to be hired for a vice president opportunity for a smaller company—which was a better title and opportunity.

Most important, apply for positions even if it's a long shot. Stretch yourself and reach a little. Be prepared for rejection and hope for an interview. Make the effort and you may be surprised with success.

The Over Qualified Resume

What if you're over-qualified for a position that you want to be interviewed for? What changes do you need to make if it's pretty clear from your experience that you're taking a step backward in your career?

You would think it would be easy to get an interview for a position you could do in your sleep. But that's the problem. Employers don't want someone who's going to get bored, isn't excited about the position, wants too much money, or worse, will leave as soon as something better comes along. All of these things may be true, but to get the interview you have to convince an employer that you really want the job and that you represent a great deal for the employer—not a risk.

So start at the beginning. Before you start your resume develop your explanation and stories about why you want the job. For example, you like being a manager and you'd like to be a manager again someday, but you miss the excitement of being in the trenches. Or you've wanted for years to branch out into a new area, or the field you've been working in is going away or downsizing.

You have to know how you're going to deal with concerns and objections before you even start your resume. Your resume needs to carefully lay out your qualifications for the job, without overstating it. You won't get a job that you're over-qualified for by making the case that you're over-qualified.

So how do you approach this task? Here are some suggestions:

- Follow the job requirements. Show that you've done the tasks the employer is looking for; that you've supervised, helped customers or whatever it is that the employer's identified in the job posting. If they're looking for a supervisor don't tell them about the executive role you had. The decision-maker doesn't want the competition, and believe it or not, former executives are not always great supervisors. Don't emphasize your ability to make big decisions if the job doesn't require big decisions to be made. If you want to get an interview, first and

foremost you have to look like the employee they want to hire.
- Dumb down your titles. I've had the luxury of having multiple titles in many of my positions and the ability to make up titles in some of my jobs. When I'm modifying my resume I'll pick the title that accurately describes what I did, but also aligns to the position I want to interview for. I've been an officer for several small companies I've worked for but when I apply for manager jobs, often with bigger companies, I leave off the officer titles and stick with the simplest title I can. Don't lie about what you did, but potential employers rarely check beyond the names of past employers, time periods and to confirm the general job descriptions.
- Focus on the duties and accomplishments that align with the new position. You may have led a multi-million dollar project but if that experience indicates that you're over-qualified don't include it, or modify it to be less pretentious. Remember that your resume is a marketing brochure; you get to choose which qualifications and accomplishments to focus on—so pick the attributes that the employer is looking for.
- Be humble. I've seen numerous resumes where the applicant clearly wanted me to know that he or she was over-qualified. Employers don't want candidates who start the process with an attitude. Having extra experience can be a real bonus for an employer, but to get an interview you have to demonstrate you can do the job and that you want it.

It's not fun to need a job so bad that you have to backtrack to find one. We'd all like our careers to progress to the top – and as quickly as possible. But when you find yourself applying for jobs where you're over-qualified, make sure your focus is on what the employer wants and needs; not on your need to let the world know that you're better than the position.

Resume Issues

Sometimes you have issues you can't gloss over in a resume that makes it more difficult for you to get interviews—or a job. These include a lack of education, unusual career changes, self-employment, unemployment, medical issues, or age. None of these issues are insurmountable, but they can make your job search more difficult and they require careful resume preparation.

Don't cover up these problems by lying on your resume. Don't invent positions, education, or accomplishments. Resume dishonesty is grounds for termination. On the other hand, your resume is your marketing brochure and you don't have to put all of the negatives up front. Here are some thoughts on how to deal with some of the more common issues:

Lack of Education

Years ago, I had a good friend who was intelligent, very good at what she did and had responsibilities far above her title and salary. Yet she couldn't get promoted or find a position that matched her skills because she didn't have a college degree. She had the skills, but the next level up the ladder uniformly required a four-year degree. Because of family circumstances she didn't feel she could start school.

Her solution was to develop a plan that included earning a professional designation to help bridge the degree gap. In addition she took finance and business classes at a community college. But the real focus of her strategy was a resume and marketing plan that emphasized her skills and her accomplishments.

She focused her resume and marketing material on her performance, senior level responsibilities and her impact. She was able to show she was capable of handling a management position. She created a portfolio of marketing materials: samples of letters, reports and presentations. She put together a list of prestigious references to support her experience. She worked hard to get around the HR representatives so she could meet directly with decision-makers. The job hunt took longer, but in the end, she got a great management position.

Self-Employment

Self-employment can be a challenge in getting hired because businesses sometimes look at self-employment as less demanding or are concerned that as an employee you'll work for a few years and then leave and take valuable customers with you.

I've worked with people trying to return to employment after several years of self-employment and all of them had difficulty getting interviews and figuring out how to sell themselves in their resumes. Their problems seemed to be a combination of standing out from the normal job pool and rusty job hunting skills.

Here are suggestions that may help you prepare a resume that increases your odds of being interviewed—and will help you prepare your message for those interviews.

- Don't make a big deal about the fact that you were self-employed, owned the company or that you handled everything from sweeping the floor to signing the checks. Most companies don't need people who can do everything—they want the person who fills their specific need best.
- Identify your company just like any of the companies you worked for before. Put the name of the company, a title, the time operated and location. Don't use self-employed as a position title or company name.
- Be flexible with titles and job descriptions. I worked with a person with an accounting background looking to return to a larger company after several years owning a retail business. He could have put down any title, but since he was looking for an accounting position he labeled himself the accounting manager and focused on his knowledge of accounting and retail in his resume. Don't use every experience for every employer, just those that will help you persuade an employer to interview you.
- Demonstrate the valuable lessons you learned and skills obtained that will add value to their organization. Don't

confess that you weren't successful—employers want successful employees.
- Show that you're still (or have become) a team player. Persuade employers that you're looking for stability, support, responsibility and teamwork.
- Be positive—you chose to be self-employed and now you're choosing to get a traditional job. I once interviewed a candidate who had been a consultant for several years who confessed that he became a consultant after being let go and now wanted a job because he wasn't very good at marketing his consulting services. It was all true, but it wasn't a very persuasive sales pitch!

Periods of Unemployment

Gaps in employment occur for lots of reasons. You need to cover or explain gaps in your resume because noticeable gaps can create concerns that may lead to rejection of your resume.

There are ways to gloss over smaller gaps, including listing periods of employment in years rather than months. For example, "January 2001 to January 2003," followed by "January 2004 to January 2008" becomes "2001–2003" followed by "2004–2008." An interviewer can't tell from your resume that there was a gap. You may have to fill in the gaps when they come up in an interview, but at least they won't be an impediment to getting an interview.

The problem is obviously magnified if a gap lasts years instead of months. The longer the gap, the bigger the problem, because big employment gaps may have been caused by problems or situations you don't want to share with an interviewer.

You have several options in dealing with gaps in employment. One is to give your gap its own name or identity. If that period were a business, what would it have been called? What were your responsibilities and what did you learn that you can bring to the workplace? This works well if you're a homemaker returning to the workforce; pointing out your skills and accomplishments.

This approach can also work for periods of personal growth: walking around the world, writing a book, time in a monastery, returning to school. Life-changing experiences are also usually life-enriching and life-improving experiences. You just need to convince employers that you're a stable employee.

Another option is to leave dates off the resume. While this method hides the gaps, it can cause concern because it's a red flag that there *are* gaps.

A third option is to put the dates in and simply leave the gap there. Gaps before your last employment are often not noticed in the initial screening process unless the company uses software that's designed to flag all potential gaps. Screeners, and even managers, will not always do a calculation of employment dates. If you don't treat a gap as a significant issue they might not either.

Except for entry-level positions, if you're coming back from an extended period of unemployment you'll need to have an explanation. Prepare your story of why the gap is there, why it's justified and why it doesn't impact your ability to add value and help the employer. If you find you're not getting a response from your resumes you'll probably have to explain the issue in your resume or cover letter.

Job Hopping

The opposite of a gap is having too many jobs in a short period of time. Job-hopping indicates to employers that an applicant lacks discipline, has employment problems or has a short attention span. An excessive number of different employers will raise eyebrows.

If you've had multiple employers over the past couple of years for reasons beyond your control, it's a good idea to explain what happened in the job descriptions. Don't let an employer make the wrong assumption. Tell them if the position was eliminated, was temporary when you were hired, or if the company had issues such as bankruptcy.

Of course, if you've had lots of jobs because you really do have a short attention span or authority issues that's a different problem. Eventually, job hopping without realistic explanations will prevent you from getting interviews. In a tight job market, employers can be picky, eliminating applicants who don't have sticking power—companies hate turnover. If you have a problem sticking with employment, consider reexamining your decisions and career choices. Figure out what *you* need to change.

It should be obvious, but don't lie on your resume. I've been involved in a couple of situations where candidates left employers off their resume—usually because they were let go. If a potential employer runs a credit or background check, they'll usually find these omitted employers. In the cases I was involved in, offers were withdrawn and in one instance the new employee was let go immediately.

Medical Issues

Medical issues become a problem in a resume when they've caused employment gaps or job-hopping. Your resume is your marketing brochure, so you're allowed to downplay significant health issues. In rare cases, overcoming an illness may be something you want to include if you can create a strength out of the experience, or if that experience is actually desirable for a job—such as a counselor for patients with similar issues.

If you can do the job, don't include medical problems in your resume. If you can add value, you need to be able to make your case in person. If it's in your resume, preconceptions can eliminate you as a candidate before the interview ever begins.

Some medical issues are protected by the local or Federal laws. Including these problems in a resume is a good way to get screened out—it may be a technical violation, but it's hard to prove and employers want to avoid litigation that could be more viable after interviewing or hiring you.

Age Issues

A good friend recently found himself looking for work after several decades with the same company—during which time he had worked his way up to be a senior executive, only to be "realigned" to a senior management position when the company was acquired by a large international organization. After a few more corporate alignments, he was let go. He was approaching retirement but wanted to work for a few more years and he had a huge wealth of experience and skills to bring to a new company.

He had two problems: how to explain his demotion and his age, which was apparent from college dates and his years of employment. I asked him how he dealt with these issues in his resume and he had some pretty good suggestions to share with you.

- *Use a Limited Number of Job Titles.* Over thirty years he had over a dozen different titles with different departments. In preparing his resume he picked the three titles that were closest to the type of position he was looking for—and pretty sure he could compete for. He wasn't looking to be a senior executive for a large company, so he didn't use that title.
- *Don't Use Dates.* Dates, especially early in his career, could hurt his chance of getting an interview. While he couldn't hide his age in an interview, he wanted to be able to present his message in person. So he indicated in his job description that he had been with his last employer for more than twenty years in a variety of positions, but didn't give any specific dates. He didn't use dates for college or other positions either.
- *Use Targeted Accomplishments.* As part of his preparation he made a long list of all the things he had accomplished with the company (His inventory). The list would have filled ten pages, so he had to cut it down to the really significant accomplishments, and specifically those that would make him more attractive to his target employer. Even though he only used three titles, he picked the accomplishments from his entire career that made him look the best.
- *More Than One Employer.* There are some experts who recommend that you only go back 15 years, but he was concerned that only listing one employer would look odd. He decided to list three employers, again without dates, and his duties and accomplishments at each. He could have included two more employers but he didn't have the space, didn't think it would help and his first two jobs out of college weren't related to the field he ended up in.

Making these changes to his resume helped him get more phone calls and interviews. He believed that a couple of employers didn't hire him because of his age, but within several months of intense job hunting he got a great job with a growing company in a mentoring and technical consulting role—exactly what he was looking for.

Some of these issues will make it harder to find a job. You need to do what you can to present the best case for what you bring to an employer. You need to know what you bring to the table then put together the best marketing presentation you can in your resume and cover letter.

Make it easy for the employer to see how you meet their needs and can solve their problems. Make sure that your resume is professional and well-written. Keep sending it out so you can get the interviews that will lead to a job offer.

The Cover Letter

For most professional positions, a cover letter is expected. Even when applying online, include a cover letter when you can. Always follow-up by sending both a cover letter and a resume in the mail if you can figure out who to send it to. A cover letter should be short, professional and informative; introducing your resume and asking for an interview.

The theme of your cover letter is what you can do for the recipient. You're trying to persuade the reader that you meet their needs. While your letter should introduce your resume, make sure you don't repeat the whole resume. Use the job post and the summary section of your resume as resources for your letter. I sometimes use the job description as a template for my cover letter, pasting the job description in my letter and writing around the key words and following its organization.

Another purpose of a cover letter can be to explain why you're applying for a stretch position, a position in an unrelated field or one that requires education or experience you don't have. In one or two paragraphs explain how your experience has prepared you to help their organization. Don't write a novel and don't beg.

Sometimes you can use your cover letter to explain unusual circumstances. During one job hunt I heard from a recruiter that it looked like I had been job hopping for the last several years, when really I had followed a senior executive to several companies at his request. I began using my cover letters to explain my job changes—and invited the readers to contact the executive for references.

One common omission from cover letters is to forget the main purpose of the resume—to ask for an interview. Don't be afraid to ask for an appointment. The best way is to end the letter with something like this:

> *"I appreciate your time reading my resume. I can add value to your organization in this role and I am confident that you will find it worth your time to interview me for this position. I look forward to meeting with you."*

Or you can use a more direct approach:

"I have the skills you are looking for. I am confident that I can demonstrate my value in an interview and I am requesting an opportunity to meet you. I look forward to your contact so we can set up an interview."

One of the most important principles of sales is to ask for the sale. If you believe you can solve an employer's problem, ask for the chance to prove it.

Last, edit and proofread your cover letter. Run it by your editors, read it aloud and read it backwards (paragraph by paragraph). Don't let a cover letter go out with spelling or grammar errors. Make sure it looks professional and that it matches your resume in style and layout.

REFERENCES

References are an interesting part of the job-hunting process these days. Most employers ask for them, but never call them and are cynical about their value. The most effective references are from people the decision-maker knows or current employees of the potential employer.

Your resume or cover letter should offer to provide references if they're wanted. Bring your best references with you when you interview. Before you interview, try to determine if you know anyone that the decision-makers know, Linked-in and similar services can be a valuable resource in finding connections when you know who you're going to interview with.

Once you know that references are going to be required, contact your potential references to make sure they're willing to provide a reference—and that they're going to say something positive about you.

On two occasions I've been used as a reference without notice. The first time wasn't an issue, I gave a great reference for a friend; it was just a surprise. The second time was a problem, not only was it a surprise but I didn't like the person. She hadn't been a good employee and hadn't left under good circumstances. I was put into an awkward position and while I didn't criticize her, I wasn't positive about her and I did tell the potential employer that I was surprised I was being used as a reference.

Make sure your references help you. Pick them carefully, be sure they can communicate well and are prepared to answer questions about you. Most important, make sure they like you.

Another thing you can do is to have a reference letter to take with you or to provide after an interview. When I ask someone to provide a letter of reference, I usually prepare a letter and ask if they'll sign it. My references aren't offended as long as it accurately reflects our relationship and experience. So be proactive and prepare a letter you can give to a potential employer.

Successful Interviews

INTERVIEWING STRATEGY

It's not enough to show up for an interview and hope it goes well. The job interview is so much more important than your resume in actually getting an offer. Your resume gets you an interview, but the interview is where decisions are made about who to hire.

Your strategy is your plan of how you're going to look, answer questions, act, interact and ask questions. Your focus is to sell your ability to help the employer solve their problems. This is an important point that I make many times in this book—*the job hunting process isn't about you*! To be successful you have to focus on how you can help employer.

Your strategy for interviewing starts with your resume. Your resume should reflect your marketing message and highlight your strengths. It should include information that's designed to lead to questions about your experience and skills. If you make a claim that you saved an employer a million dollars, you need to be ready to explain how you did it!

You have to be prepared to answer the questions that are likely to be asked. For technical jobs you have to be able to answer the technical questions. Any qualification in the job description and everything on your resume is fair game for interview questions. In addition there are the standard questions about your strengths, weaknesses, failures and dreams that are included in all the books about interviewing. You know these questions are coming, so know how to answer them.

For example, a common interview question is what do you want to be doing in five years? I've had interviewees tell me they want to be in my job, they want to be president of the company or they want to make money and travel the world. I understand these were truthful answers, but they aren't answers that help me want to hire these candidates.

What's the right answer to this kind of question? I usually explain that I have trouble knowing what'll happen over the next five years, but I want to be happy knowing I've contributed to the company's success and I hope there are opportunities for personal and career growth. I try to emphasize that I have goals and can think long-term, but that my focus is on being successful in helping the company. Never forget that you're trying to make a sale of your ability to help the decision-makers look brilliant for hiring you.

Being successful in interviewing is about knowing what you want to say and then practicing saying it. Your interview strategy is your message, your marketing materials and your preparation to present that message. If you're not getting invited back for the final interview rounds you need to evaluate your strategy and answers. Get feedback from recruiters and interviewers about what you could improve and issues that you didn't resolve. Be proactive, keep getting interviews and you'll make that sale.

ANSWERING QUESTIONS

Your resume earns you an invitation to compete in the race—interviews are the race itself. Employers interview to measure candidates. Decision-makers try to evaluate the ability, credibility and value of the candidates in this peculiar process. It's essential that you get an invitation to participate and once you're there you have to finish strong in every round.

If you've been through enough interviews, you know that they usually consist of familiar questions. Anticipating what you'll be asked isn't that difficult, so there's no excuse for not being prepared for most of the questions you'll get. Don't wait until you're in the interview to start formulating answers!

Answering interview questions is like taking a test in school, an open book test because you know most of the questions. There are no "wrong" answers—just *your* answers. The way to prepare is to know your message, have stories to tell and practice answering actual questions. Review your resume and the job post, and think about the questions that you would ask.

Most candidates try too hard. They think they have to hit a home run with every question. Just answer every question, stick to your message and move the process forward. The more pressure you put on yourself, the worse you'll do.

A good answer has three elements:
- It answers the question that was asked;
- It explains your value to that employer; and,
- It uses simple stories to demonstrate your value.

So how do you do this? Practice answering as many questions as you can find before you ever get to an interview. Read books about interviewing; books written for job hunters and for employers. Review the questions in these books and make sure you can answer them. You're not trying to memorize hundreds of answers to questions that may never be asked. You're practicing answering and telling your stories to ensure a great interview experience.

Two Minute Answers

Don't ramble or go longer than two minutes unless you're talking about their issues. Even then, don't do all the talking; ask questions and let your interviewers participate. As an interviewer, I liked to hand candidates a list of twenty questions to answer without interruption. It's amazing how often candidates just ramble instead of answering the questions. Candidates fail because they aren't prepared to just answer questions.

When you practice answering questions use a timer to see how long you're taking. Another good way to practice this is to join Toastmasters and participate in Table Topics where you practice giving two minute spontaneous speeches. Don't let yourself just go on and on. Answer the question and stop talking.

Be Positive

Even to negative questions. For example, if you're asked about your last boss's weakness, don't answer that he was a complete loser. Give a simple answer and stick to your message—which should be that you're a team player.

"My last manager was the best technical manager I've ever had, but he had problems communicating his expectations. I was able to work with him, define my responsibilities and we got along great."

Stay away from personal confessions or societal gripes. That's not your message and it won't get you invited back. Employers don't want to hire a complainer. Don't complain, whine or share your intimate thoughts.

Stay on message

This means you need to have a message. Have your sales pitch ready—what you've done, the skills you have and what you can do for that employer. Everything else is fluff.

Have stories to tell. They're the best way to make a point, because people remember stories. For each skill you want to sell, have an experience that illustrates it. It doesn't have to be a "he said-she said" kind of story. Stories should be examples of hard experiences, trials overcome, great customer service, solving problems, achieving goals and the greatest moments of your career. You should have about twenty of these stories that illustrate your strengths, and weaknesses. It's easier to remember stories than pat answers, and with practice you'll be able to remember twenty or more good stories you can use over and over again.

Be Professional—Be Yourself

Don't be buddies with the interviewers. Stay calm, be professional. Act like you've been in an interview before. There are no right answers; there are just *your* answers—your very well-prepared answers.

There are books that give you "great" answers to normal interview questions. These answers can give you ideas and help you prepare your responses, but don't memorize them. They aren't your answers. It'll be obvious if you try to memorize someone else's responses. You need to come up with your own answers, your message and your stories.

Here's a common interview question: *"What was the most frustrating thing about your last job?"*

I've heard canned answers that the interviewee's biggest frustration was not being able to work longer and harder – this is a nonsense answer that interviewers will see through. You need an answer identifying something that was frustrating but that won't alienate the interviewer, and then practice telling the story about how you overcame the challenge.

I have two stories that help me respond to this type of question. One is about a company I joined because of a training program that was highly regarded in my industry. Three months after I joined the company, they suspended the program and never restarted it—which really was very frustrating. Then I tell the interviewer how I completed a professional program instead. The story answers the question and demonstrates my commitment to personal development.

My second story involves a company I joined with significant financial problems. I was brought in to help solve the problems but could never get the Board and executive management to take the necessary steps. I learned a lot in that position, but it was frustrating to work with leadership who wanted different results without changing what they were doing!

Here's another question that often comes up: *"Where do you see yourself in five years?"*

I answer this question by reflecting on where I was five years ago, when I was committed to an employer without a clue that I was going to be searching for a job now. I point out that the future is hard to predict, and I focus on what, not where, I want to be.

"It's hard to know where any of us will be in five years, but I do know what I want to be. I want to be an expert in my field, a resource and leader in my company. I want to be known for my commitment to performance and profitability. Wherever I am, I want to be a loyal and valued member of a team that has fun and is successful."

Stick to your message—no matter what the question is. Some experts suggest ignoring the question and answering the question you wish had been asked. I don't advocate ignoring the question, but it's okay to change the focus of the question.

Here are questions that you ought to be prepared to answer. How will *you* answer them and stay on message? Answer the question, sell your value and tell your story.

- What were your expectations with your previous employers?
- What were your responsibilities?
- What major challenges and problems did you face?
- How did you handle them?
- What were the best/worst aspects of each position?
- What were your biggest accomplishments and failures?
- Why and how did you leave each employer?
- How do you feel about your last job responsibilities?
- What motivates you to do a great job?
- Tell me about going "out on a limb" to get a job done.

For more practice, review the questions in Appendix 3.

Not all interview questions will make sense to you when you're being interviewed, and some questions are designed to fluster you. The interview is a game where the employer wants to see the "real" person, so let them see the real, and very prepared, you!

Dealing with Stress

Be prepared for pressure in an interview. There are ways to deal with it, the worst of which are a drink or medication right before an interview. The two best ways I have found of dealing with stress and pressure in any situation are to be over-prepared—through practice—and to have a ritual or technique to relax yourself.

Have a ritual and make it part of every performance—including practice—so your brain associates success with the ritual. Right before the interview begins I hold my breath . . . I take a deep breath and hold it for a slow ten count and then slowly let it out. I also do it when I practice. When I'm waiting for an interviewer to arrive, I can hold my breath, let it out and then I'm ready to perform. Other examples of rituals: tensing all your muscles for a five count, flexing muscles or rubbing your neck, forehead or palms. Don't get in the habit of doing it during the interview; you don't want to create a nervous habit. Your ritual should be something you do right before the interview or practice session—a trigger for your subconscious that you're ready to go.

PREPARE, PREPARE, PREPARE

One of the secrets to a great interview is to be prepared. Successful preparation can take hours of work. There are things you can do—should do, have to do—to be prepared and to feel confident.

You want to know as much as you can about the hiring process, the company, the position, competitors and the people you'll meet while interviewing. You can get this information from a variety of sources including professional contacts, the internet, media and from people you know.

The Hiring Process

Ask the employer when you're first contacted what their interviewing process is. Always ask for as much information as they'll provide, such as how many rounds there are and who you'll be meeting with at each stage. Ask for the names, departments and titles of each of the interviewers. If you're being brought in for multiple interviews, ask for a schedule of the day and the names of the interviewers. Don't be afraid to ask questions about what's going to happen and when.

A word of caution: don't hold a company to the time frames they give you. Candidates get frustrated when they're not called back when they were told it would happen. I know from experience as both a decision-maker and a candidate that it usually takes longer than expected for a company to make decisions. Managers try to set a target date, but things happen. It's alright to contact someone if you don't hear back, but don't be demanding or express frustration. Be patient.

The Company

A good place to start researching a company is their website. Read everything there. If they have copies of recent financial statements, read them. Even if you don't think you'll need to know their financial numbers, you can get a lot of information from an annual report, including messages from the senior executives about goals, new projects and initiatives. Pay attention to information about the company's history, mission and values.

Find out what others are reporting about the organization. Look for profiles or articles about the organization in national or local media. Are there issues of concern that may come up in an interview? When you've done your homework about a company, it will show and it makes a great impression.

The Position

Study the job description. Review the requirements and described duties and make sure that you understand all of the terms and acronyms used. If they want someone familiar with PTAT, you need to know what it means. If you know someone who has a similar position at a different company, call them and find out what the job entails.

The Competitors

Spend time finding out who the potential employer's competition is, especially if your future department produces a product or service and has strong competition. Look at the competition's websites (check to see if they have any open positions!) and get informed about their products and marketing. You never know when being prepared to talk about a specific competitor will give you an edge over another candidate.

The Interviewers

Find out about the people you'll be meeting. Check for profiles on professional networks, which provide basic background, education and accomplishments. You're not doing a background check on them, but you do want to humanize your interviewers and find things in common—education, military service or previous shared employers. Don't make a big deal that you did a lot of research, but if you find information that can help you to connect with an interviewer, bring it up or look for opportunities to discuss it during the interview.

Knowing more will help you prepare and relax, because there are fewer unknowns about the organization and the people you'll be meeting.

BE ORGANIZED

Your job search will be easier and more successful if you learn to stay organized. Keep track of what you do, what you send out and everything you learn. Don't trust your memory when it comes to what you sent out and what has happened.

Save every resume you send out—on your computer or in a file. Everything related to an application should be saved in one place: the original job post, e-mails, research, your resume and your notes. If you're using a computer, e-mails and websites can be printed to a PDF format and saved. If you're using paper, make sure you save a copy of every resume you send out and create a folder or binder for each job you interview for. Don't assume that the job post will still be there in a couple of months when they call you in for an interview. You want to be able to open your folder and spend five minutes reviewing the contents, not hours recreating the original information and your material.

I have a couple of tools I use. I have a folder in my documents section on my computer and I create a new sub-folder for every employer I contact. In each sub-folder I include job-post, emails and research about the company. Because I submit tailored resumes for each position, I keep the resume and cover letter in the subfolder. I also print pages from websites and my research. My goal is to be able to immediately find and use the information I collect. When I get a call from the company I can immediately pull up the post and the information I sent them to ensure that I stay on message and look brilliant!

When I'm engaged in a full-time job search I also have a spreadsheet with different tabs. I have one tab with a list of companies and recruiter sites I want to monitor. I look at these sites once a week.

I have another tab with my current active applications where I include notes about contacts and dates to follow up. I also include ID's and passwords if I had to register to apply.

I have another tab of positions that have passed me over – my "NO" list. It's important to keep track of positions and employers that you've applied to and where you may have had contact with someone in case you want to apply for another position with the same company.

And last, I have a tab for companies that I've contacted with a resume and cover letter—my marketing list. I send out a couple of letters a day and then follow up with individuals I've sent resumes to.

Whenever I have an interview I print my resume, cover letter, the job post and my notes and put them in a folder to take with me. The folder allows me to have quick access to information through multiple rounds of interviews. After I accept a position the folder becomes my new employment file. If I don't get the job I save my information on the computer, in case the company has another opening or contacts me later—which has happened.

These are only suggestions. How you track information is up to you. Just make sure you're organized and consistent. Some people use computer databases or spreadsheets as a tool to track resumes and materials. Documents can be organized or linked to a central location and even indexed so you can use them again for similar employers.

Get organized so you don't waste a lot of time recreating the wheel every time an employer calls you or you need to know what you've done with a company. Keep your system simple so you won't spend more time organizing than selling yourself.

Having a system will help you stay busy and moving forward. And moving forward will ensure you succeed.

TELL STORIES

If you want to be remembered you have to tell stories. It's not enough to answer questions; you have to give examples that add credibility to your responses and that make your answers—and you—more memorable.

After interviewing multiple candidates, I've often had trouble remembering the people I interviewed. It was the stories that I remembered. Great stories make an impression. Great stories, well told, with enthusiasm and a smile can turn you into a great candidate!

Your Stories

The first thing you have to do is to come up with the stories you want to tell. It's not enough to tell a potential employer that you're organized. If you want to stand out and be remembered you should have a story about a time when you organized an office or project, how you did it and the impact it had.

Look at your resume. You've developed a message and you've chosen to focus on certain skills and experiences. Write down the situations and events you were thinking about when you created your resume. Review some of the common interview questions in this book and that you've collected and think of the stories you told to answer these questions, or that you would tell if you're asked these questions.

In an interview you want to tell stories that support your marketing message. So you want to focus on stories that demonstrate your skills, your experience and your value.

One of the themes I develop in my resume is the ability to manage crises situations. I have a couple of great stories I tell about problems that threatened previous employers. In my resume I briefly reference these events and I include them in my cover letter. These are stories about problems that seemed insurmountable and how I managed resources and people to get the best possible result.

I have stories about dealing with difficult people, persuading people to change, helping difficult employees, difficult bosses, why I left previous employers, and stories to talk about my weaknesses.

In all I have about twenty stories I've developed for most interview questions and maybe another twenty stories that I occasionally use for specific kinds of questions.

This may seem like a lot of stories to remember, but the great thing about stories is that they're easier to remember than technical answers—especially because they're *your* stories.

The Interview Story

So what's the difference between an answer and a story? The difference is how you tell it, the words you use and the mental images you create.

An interview story is a little different from the stories you tell in other settings. It has a purpose and it should have a structure. The purpose is to answer a question and demonstrate your strengths and abilities. The structure is tight, active and short. All answers in an interview should be around two minutes – and stories are no different.

Here's the interview question, *"Tell me about your ability to manage during a crisis"*. Your interview answer might be something like this.

> *In 2004, I managed my department when our computer system failed. We lost all our data and spent several weeks recreating the data while servicing our clients. I reported to senior management on a regular basis and we were able to get up and running within 3 weeks by working long hours and weekends. I was recognized by the President of the company for our efforts and my leadership.*

This is a great answer, and the kind of experience you should be prepared to talk about. But it could be so much better, and make you memorable as a leader with a little story telling. Here's the story that answers the same question.

> *In September of 2004, right after Labor Day weekend, we were getting ready to go home after a long day when all the computers made this noise and died. I don't know if you've*

ever had that experience, but it was a little surreal, all of the monitors flashed and then went out like a bad horror movie. We tried to find a simple explanation for what was happening—hoping for the best but fearing that it was a big problem.

It was the worst of all the possible situations. We had lost all of our data: client lists, notes and calendars. We were a service department without a clue of what we were supposed to be doing on Wednesday morning, and I was in charge of minimizing the damage, rebuilding our department and providing the service we had a reputation for providing while IT restored our system.

I was there until 2 am, meeting with IT, figuring out what tools we had and coming up with a plan. I brought the supervisors in at 6 am the next morning and by the time the staff showed up we had a plan. We had assignments and we went to work. It took three weeks to get back up and going. We pulled a couple of all-nighters reconstructing our information from financial records, what data we could recover and everyone's notes. We came up with procedures for communicating with our clients and dealing with emergencies as they came up. And we doubled the profitability of the local pizza place.

I don't know whether I was more proud the day I realized that we had not only survived but that we'd done it in style; or at the end the year when I accepted an award from the president of the company on behalf of the department for what we had accomplished. It was an emergency that could have crippled our company, and it should have taken months to get back on track. Because of good people, great support, planning, discipline and sacrifice we did the almost impossible.

This is a story. It provides context, drama and a happy ending. You can tell it with enthusiasm and it will be remembered. The listener can relate to the problem and how you led the resolution. And it allows you to not only highlight your strengths and accomplishments, but share the credit with others.

It takes time to develop good stories and practice delivering them. Some suggestions as you develop your interview stories:

- Don't hog the credit. Nobody believes stories where you singlehandedly saved the company while rebuilding the building and taking on the competition in hand-to-hand combat . . . It's enough to have done your part well and it reflects well on you that you can give credit to others. It's a good thing to have managed and worked with sharp people.
- You can keep stories shorter and more powerful by adding details that the listener can relate to. I added the fact that the failure took place right after Labor Day and at the end of the day because we can all relate to coming back from a long weekend or vacation to a huge crisis. I don't have to add a lot of words to describe the emotional context if I can find simple, short facts that the interviewer can relate to.
- Bring the story back to your point. This is a story that you're telling to answer an interview question. Don't lose sight of where you are, what the question is, and what you're trying to accomplish with your answer.
- Don't share confidential information. If explaining why the computers crashed is embarrassing to a former employer or would give inappropriate information, don't use those details.
- Don't be negative about people in your stories. Even when talking about bad bosses or problem customers, don't lash out at the people you're talking about. No potential employer wants to be the subject of your next story about a bad boss! You can tell stories about issues, problems, misunderstandings and conflicts without attacking people.

Telling Stories

Storytelling is an art. It requires time to develop stories and it takes practice to deliver them well. Storytelling helps the listener connect to what you're talking about by adding context, color, conflict and closure.

Context. Context is defined as the conditions where something occurs. In a story, context is the facts that help the listener understand the size and depth of the issues of the story.

For example, I can tell you that my plane arrived late last night so I'm tired. But it's the context that helps you feel something—the story about how I left yesterday morning at 5 am for an early meeting, I missed my scheduled flight back, I was on standby and couldn't get on the next flight, and finally how I was the last passenger on the last flight and that we hit bad weather on the way back. Now you can relate to my experience. The context helps you relate to how I felt, because you've been there and suddenly it's not just that I arrived late last night.

Good story telling is adding context with the fewest possible facts. By finding elements that other people can relate to you can add context without long explanations. One of the stories I tell in interviews is about when an employer brought everyone into the lunch room and announced that we were being terminated, that all our jobs were being restructured and that we'd be able to apply for the new jobs. I start the story by telling them about "Black Tuesday", which is what we all called that memorable day. Just this title creates a context that the listener can relate to and an emotional framework for the story.

How much context you need depends on the story and the point you're trying make. If people you tell the story to don't get the point you probably need some more context.

Color. Color is adding details that help you visualize or experience the story through your other senses. If I told you that on "Black Tuesday" the meeting was called before lunch and someone was cooking spaghetti in the microwave you can recreate the smell of the room. If I tell you that 80 people were crammed into a room that comfortably fit 40 you can relate to being cramped and uncomfortable

If I tell you that on my flight last night someone got sick on the plane because of turbulence, you immediately have a sensory reaction—but probably not a good one; so be careful about the color you add to your stories.

Conflict. Conflict is the opposition of actions, options, ideas or choices. It's the heart of the story, the tension and the reason you're using the story to answer an interview question. The conflict helps you show how you've overcome obstacles, how you've worked with people, or how you identified and are correcting your weaknesses.

In my "Black Tuesday" story, the conflict is that we'd all been terminated, but we were expected to go back to work and make significant decisions for the good of the company! I talk about the home office VIP ending the meeting by explaining that we should all go back to work and that we'd get receive further instructions over the next few weeks. I was managing a small team and there was a lot of anger and frustration when most of my team came back after lunch; and not everyone came back.

The conflict doesn't have to be huge, but it has to be real: a decision point, a problem or a situation that required your skills and experience to deal with.

Closure. I use my "Black Tuesday" story to illustrate how I dealt with a bad situation, managed my team and got results. The closure is that I provided leadership and helped people adapt to stress and an unusual situation. In you conclusion, you want to come back to your message of how you can help a new employer; with what you learned from the challenges you've faced in the past.

Your story's closure should demonstrate your skills, yet still be responsive to the question. "Black Tuesday" is a great story because I can talk about leadership, dealing with a crisis, helping a team stay focused, and I even used it as an example of how I've dealt with poor management. Your stories can, and should, be used for answering a variety of questions—but always to help decision-makers remember you and the skills and solutions you can bring to their organization.

PRACTICE, PRACTICE, PRACTICE

You're prepared, you have your message, you have stories and you're organized. Now you need to put it all together and develop your interviewing skills.

Answering interview questions is a specific skill. I know from experience that it has to be developed. Over the years I have interviewed many skilled professionals. While many of them were good at talking, most of them weren't that great at answering interview questions.

To get the necessary experience to be a great interviewee you have two choices—have lots of actual interviews or practice answering interview questions lots of times. Actual interviews are great practice. You can also get the experience you need in practice interviews and learn more in the process because you can get immediate feedback in a practice interview.

There's no short-cut or secret tip I can give you to becoming a successful interviewee. Becoming more comfortable being interviewed happens when you're familiar with the interview questions, you know your message and you can consistently give good answers. It requires practice and consistent, intentional work to get better.

Going through one practice interview will make you more comfortable with the process; going through ten practice interviews will help you develop answers; doing a hundred practice interviews will make you a great interviewee.

Here are the things you should focus on to become a great interviewee.

Make Your Practice Real

Don't sit in your living room having someone half-heartedly ask you questions. Find a quiet place and choose someone who's willing to ask you interview questions, listen and give you feedback.

For practice interviews I like to go to friends' offices. I ask if they're willing to meet me over lunch, early in the morning or at the end of the day. I don't want to interrupt their office or schedule, but being in a real business setting gives a practice interview a realistic feeling.

My second favorite location is a study room at the local library. They're easy to reserve during the day and provide a quiet conference room setting. Whatever location you chose, make sure it's away from distractions and interruptions. Choosing a public place can be distracting and inhibiting, so unless your real interviews are going to be in a restaurant, don't practice there!

Pick a variety of people to be your interviewers, not just the business people you know. Interviewers and decision-makers come in all shapes, sizes and types. Anyone can help you as an interviewer and you'll be surprised who gives you the best feedback and suggestions. Reach out to former colleagues and even bosses; include interviewers who have interviewing experience and some that don't. If you join job hunting groups you can ask the other participants to interview you—and return the favor.

Go through twenty to thirty questions in a practice interview. You can make it easier on your interviewer by providing interview questions. Bring a copy of your resume and if you're getting ready for a specific interview bring a copy of the job post. Encourage your interviewer to ask follow-up questions and to ask you to clarify answers that don't make sense. Sometimes you can ask interviewers to go hard on you, asking tough questions or being a confrontational—it's good to have some practice with interviews that don't go well.

Take the Practice Seriously

The more you can simulate an actual interview, the more prepared you'll be. Dress for an interview so you know your suit fits, looks good and that you can think while wearing a tie (for the guys). Just because it's practice doesn't mean you slouch in your shorts in the living room with the television on. Pay attentions to how you sit. Don't use notes, don't call time-out, and don't have food or drink that you won't have in an interview. Make it as real as possible so when you get into a real interview it will feel like you've been there before.

Develop a Ritual

A ritual is a habit or physical action that you can use to control your stress in a real interview. It's a distinct mental or physical exercise that allows you to focus better before performing. It's very intentional. It should be done before the start of the interview; not before answering each question. And it should be part of your practice so it's effective during a real interview.

Elite athletes often use the power of a ritual before they have to perform. For example, football kickers have a specific routine they follow before kicking the ball. They take a specific number of steps, in a set pattern before kicking the ball. Basketball players may spin the ball or dribble the ball before attempting a free throw. They use this same ritual in practice and in the game—every time they perform the action.

A ritual can be any action that's intentional and helps you reduce stress. It could be applying pressure to body part, your arm, leg, or finger. It could be rubbing your hair, meditating for a few seconds or a song that you sing mentally or hum softly. Whatever it is, it needs to be part of your performance routine. Before you start an interview, you complete your ritual to get yourself ready to perform.

My ritual is to take a deep, deep breath . . . hold it as long as I can . . . and then to slowly let it out. I perform this ritual while I'm waiting in a room or in the elevator if I'm alone. This isn't something I do in front of interviewers. When I have the opportunity it's an exercise that increases my oxygen and it's a signal to my brain because I use it before practice interviews and professional presentations. It's my personal "it's show time" signal—and it works.

One important note—there's a huge difference between a stress reducing ritual and a nervous habit. A ritual is intentional. A habit happens when you're not paying attention. Habits include chewing your lips, playing with hair, flipping pens or playing with keys or personal belongings. Try to be aware of distracting habits and get rid of them.

Videotape Your Practice Interviews

Videotape your practice interviews and watch yourself. How are you sitting? Are you looking at the interviewer? Are you answering the questions that are asked? Are you doing a good job talking about your skills and the value you add? Are you keeping your answers to two minutes? Do you look excited, energized and positive? Watch for nervous habits and nervous fidgeting. There are things you're doing that you're not aware of.

Watching yourself on video will be painful, but it's one of the most effective ways to see how you look. Listen to your answers and figure out what you need to work on. Watching yourself you'll be able to see the little things that can distract an interviewer, and how you can better project and physically participate in the interview.

Get Feedback

Find coaches who are willing to be honest with you and who have skills you lack. Don't keep using people who aren't better at interviewing than you are and won't tell you to quit looking at your feet. Practice is about getting better, not about reinforcing bad habits. You need people who will give you feedback and suggestions on how to be a more effective interviewee.

Practice the Hard Questions

We all like to practice what we do well, but you can get more improvement and a lot more impact from practicing the questions that you find difficult to answer. If you have a problem talking about an experience without getting emotional, then practice until you don't get emotional. When you identify a problem with a specific question or a type of questions, come up with a strategy and then practice. If there are issues you have to talk about, such as age or an observable disability, be ready to talk about them.

Practice Every Week

When I work with job hunters I recommend that they set a goal for three interviews a week. If you can't get three real interviews, make up the difference with practice interviews. Get cleaned up, get out of the house and go through the whole interview process. Then go home and watch the video, take notes and start coming up with better answers and ways to overcome distracting habits.

Practice Speaking

Find opportunities to practice speaking. I recommend joining a Toastmasters clubs; it's a great place to practice extemporaneous speaking. It's also a place to learn the mechanics of speaking and presenting yourself, to find coaches and get feedback. You can also look for opportunities to speak to professional groups and job hunting groups where you can refine your personal pitch.

Your Sales Pitch

Another thing you need to practice is giving your message. In the chapter on **Marketing Yourself** is a section about developing a sales pitch—a prepared presentation that explains who you are and what you can do for an employer. To be effective giving your sales pitch you have to practice it—over and over and over.

When I got out of high school, I sold vacuum cleaners for a summer. After casually preparing for the first appointment, and completely blowing it, I took the vacuum and the manual home and learned the presentation forwards and backwards. I made every member of my family listen to my presentation and when I was done I knew how to sell vacuums, answer questions and overcome objections. I was prepared.

Having a well prepared pitch will help you answer all the questions you're asked. It will help you fill long pauses and ensure that you focus on your message during the interview.

Help Others Practice Interviewing

One of the best ways to learn a new skill is to teach it. Become an interviewer for others who need practice—especially if they've helped you. When you're coaching someone else take notes for them. You'll be amazed at how much you learn from asking questions and listening to someone else's responses.

Learn From Real Interviews

Learn from every interview, whether real or practice. When you leave an real interview, take notes immediately—listing what worked and what didn't. Think through your responses and pick the three answers you wish you could give again. When you get home, write down your best answers to these questions and practice giving them in a mirror. The next time you have a practice interview ask your interviewer to cover these questions.

You Can't Prepare for Psychological Profiles

Many employers use personality profiles and tests for applicants. The worst thing you can do is try to guess the "right" answer. There will be times that you won't get a job because of a profile. I have two thoughts on this: One, if they're right about the personality type needed for the position and you don't pass, you probably don't want to be there. Or two, if they're wrong about the position or what they need, you don't want to work for an organization that's so dysfunctional (maybe you still do—but tough luck). This may be rationalization, but this is a part of the process you can't prepare for. You'll only hurt yourself if you try to manipulate these tests.

Your Questions

You need to be ready to ask questions. Interviewers will usually ask if you have any. Having questions will show that you're prepared and interested—so have questions ready. Take notes when you research the company. If the company recently made the news for something positive, an acquisition or new product announcement, ask about the impact of these changes. You can ask about the organization's goals, or about the position itself, such as responsibilities, challenges or how success is measured.

Don't ask about vacation time, overtime or whether they have wireless connection for your phone. Are you really going to turn down the job if they don't want you on the internet during personal time? It's about convincing them to hire you because you can help them—and even your questions to them should be focused on your desire to help them.

Preparing to Discuss Money

Inevitably the question of money, both your current or past pay and your expectations, will come up in an interview. Some interviewers ask about it in the first telephone interview, while others wait until the last interview. Most of the time, you're aware of the pay range before you apply for a job.

In some cases, the salary or wage is set, and there's nothing to negotiate. But most of the time the employer has a salary range and the question is where you fall in that range. In interviews you should focus on your value to the organization, not your salary.

Your best strategy is to try to avoid committing yourself to a number in interviews. Tell potential employers that you want a salary that's fair given the value and experience you bring to the position. If an interviewer isn't satisfied with that answer and demands a number, tell them that you expect expect to be paid close to the upper end of the salary range—unless you'll take whatever they offer.

Have a strategy before you go into an interview: how are you going to deal with questions about money? What is the salary you expect and what number will you use if the question is asked? Always give yourself some room to negotiate later, but don't pick a number so high you eliminate yourself as a candidate.

Practice talking about salary and money. Use your practice interviews to help you develop your answers. If you don't practice you run the risk of getting flustered or eliminating yourself as a candidate. Be confident but not overbearing. Try to defer discussion of salary expectations until you have an offer to respond to. But if you're forced to talk dollars, trust your instincts, be prepared and do your best.

Being prepared is the best antidote for fear, panic and the pressure of being in an interview. Practicing and improving your interviewing skills is the best way to be prepared. Practice every week in real interviews, practice interviews, at Toastmasters and when you meet people. Practice telling your stories and overcome your nervous habits. You can become a good interviewer and it's a skill that will help you for your whole career.

The Screening/Telephone Interview

Screening interviews are huge obstacles in the interviewing process and very different from the rest of the process. Initial telephone interviews are usually with a HR screener, not someone who's going to make a final decision. Screeners often know little about the position's technical requirements and sometimes they know very little about the position itself or even the industry or business!

The screener's job is to take many resumes and cut them down to a small number of applicants to submit to decision-makers. Sometimes the screener is asked by a manager to conduct initial interviews and submit notes the hiring manager uses to pick a small number of applicants to talk to personally.

To be successful in this screening process you need to communicate well, keep your answers simple, mirror the position requirements, and convey an eagerness to be considered for the position. To get through the screening process you have to be positive and enthusiastic. Here are some tips to being successful:

- Be prepared. Have a copy of the resume you sent the company, the job post and company information in front of you.
- Review the job post and make sure you understand all of the requirements, acronyms and descriptions. Be prepared to talk generally about how you meet the requirements. Your message in the screening interview is that you are a perfect fit for the position and should be advanced to interview with decision-makers.
- Have stories—short stories—prepared to show your ability to work with others and make a contribution to the company.
- Be enthusiastic. I stand for telephone interviews, which makes it easier to be energetic. Smile as you talk—the interviewer can't see you but smiling increases your enthusiasm.
- Be professional. I shave, and dress up even though I'm on the telephone. I want to convey my professionalism and I want to feel professional.

- Speak clearly. Tape yourself during practice interviews and make sure that you're easy to understand and loud enough to be heard. Avoid telephone interviews on phones with bad connections.
- Don't ramble; rambling answers are even worse on the telephone than in person. Be concise, answer the questions and talk with energy.
- Don't multitask. Turn off all the distractions around you. Close the door and don't look at unrelated stuff on your computer. Pretend you're in the same room with the interviewer and stay focused on the interview.
- Don't take care of personal business. I've talked to interviewers who had candidates use the bathroom, carry on other conversations, or had distracting noise on in the background while talking on the phone. Assume if you can hear the noise that your interviewer can hear the noise. This includes typing on the keyboard or clicking the mouse.
- Don't ask questions about job specifics, hours, benefits or pay during a screening interview—screeners don't usually have this information. Ask for information about how the interview process is structured; screeners often understand and are willing to talk about the interview process.

Many companies today have a screening process to get to the "real" interviews. If you find you're having problems advancing past the screening process, practice your phone interview skills. Make a list of the questions you're asked regularly and practice answering them. Tape your practice and listen to your answers.

Don't over-stress about these interviews. They're important—but being stressed won't help you do better—and the screener is usually not a decision-maker. Be prepared and make the case for why you should be advanced to the interviews with decision-makers.

The Interview

You're waiting in the lobby or you've been taken to a conference room. It may already feel like it's been a long day but the fun part is just beginning. You're waiting for an interview to start.

It may just be a single interview or it may be a series of interviews throughout the day. This is it. For better or worse most employers will make important decisions of whether to hire you based on a random process of questions and pressure.

But you're not worried. You're prepared for this moment. You have a message. You've practiced answering interview questions. You're dressed appropriately for the interview. You are ready!

Here are things to do to make your interviews even more successful.

Pre-Interview Planning

Some basics: eat a healthy breakfast, get enough sleep, make sure your clothes are clean and ready to go. Don't discover the night before that your suit needs to be dry-cleaned!

I always prepare an interview folder in advance with instructions on where I'm going, lists of the people I'm meeting, copies of my resume and cover letter, a copy of the job post and any other material that I think I may need in the actual interview.

Try to reduce interview day stress as much as possible. Make arrangements for care of children, pets and responsibilities in advance. If you have to travel for the interview, try to get there early and leave yourself plenty of time to catch a return flight. I hate taking a 4 am flight for a morning interview so I will fly out the night before and pay for a hotel and get a good night's sleep.

Pre-interview preparation is about planning ahead so that you arrive as good as rested, fresh and ready as you can be for the interview.

Dress for Success

Dress as well as you need to dress so that you never have to worry about how you look when you get there. I usually recommend dressing one level above what you think you need to dress. This means if the office or business is very casual, dress business casual. If the office is business casual wear a tie and sport coat. If the dress code is sport coat and tie, wear a suit.

For women, the dress code can be more complicated. There is often little difference between business casual and more formal business wear. The best advice from a very professional business woman I know is to wear well-fitting, well-made clothing. Avoid sexy or revealing clothing and don't be afraid of strong colors.

Your object is to make an impression that's consistent with your message and that allows you to focus on answering questions without concern about how you look. Nothing is more distracting to you or your interviewers than to have clothes that continually need adjusting. Think about what you'll wear long before the interview. Ask questions about dress expectations before you interview. Be professional . . . dress professional.

Use Your Ritual

In the **Practice, Practice, Practice** chapter I talk about developing a ritual, a physical action you can use to reduce stress and get yourself prepared for the inquisition. While you're waiting for an interviewer or if you have breaks between interviews you can use your ritual to get yourself into the right mindset. Your ritual links real interviews to all the practice interviews where there was no stress and you did great.

Don't perform your ritual when interviewers are there, especially if it involves strange physical actions or noises. Don't make your ritual so easy that it turns into a bad habit during the interview.

Perform

An interview is a performance. It's like improvisational theater where everyone knows the theme but the actual script has to be developed. You know what kinds of questions will be asked and what tests may be given. So focus on the performance aspects of the interview.

First, be engaged. You communicate that you're engaged by making eye contact without starting a staring contest. Sit straight in your seat and lean slightly forward. When coaching public speakers I encourage them to lean forward, putting their weight on the front of their feet. When you interview you want to use the same principle. Lean forward, just a little. Turn to the person you're talking to. Use small hand gestures to make points and to bring the listener in. Demonstrate your enthusiasm and your interest by your physical presence.

Second, speak clearly. Speak strongly. Enunciate your words. Don't be too fast or too slow. Don't be artificial; it needs to be your voice and your answers.

Third, smile.

Smile

Smiling is one of the most powerful tools you have to be a great interviewee.

Smiling is powerful because when you smile, you feel less nervous. I don't know how it works, but when you smile in a high pressure situation your brain notices and it decides that if you're smiling, things can't be that bad after all. Smiling, even a faked smile, can reduce your stress, help you to be more positive and allow you to relax.

Another advantage of smiling is the impact it has on your interviewers. I have been in long, dragging interviews with candidates who won't smile—it can be painful.

Smiling breaks the ice. It creates a link with other people. It makes you less threatening and more credible. Interviewers like you when you smile and will want to work with you in the interview—not against you.

Smile, but don't laugh too much. Don't try to crack jokes or be cute. Just smile to show that you're relaxed, you're engaged, you're happy to be in the interview and you're excited to potentially be part of their organization.

Don't Stop Interviewing

As long as you're in the building or in company-provided transportation, stay in interview mode. I have heard many stories about candidates who call someone and make inappropriate comments about the interviewers or the company while in an elevator, bathroom or being driven by an employee. From the moment you enter the building to the end of the process, act like you're interviewing. Be professional with everyone, assume they will report back to the interviewers everything you say and everything you do.

The Interview Meal

The interview meal is a potential minefield. There are so many opportunities to make a mistake, embarrass yourself or get food stuck between your teeth. Meals can be a great opportunity to get to know a future employer in an informal setting—but never forget that you're still interviewing.

If you know that the interview process is going to include a meal brush up on your manners. Interviewers love to go to fancy restaurants because it's a business expense and it adds pressure. Order light healthy food and don't eat all of it. Don't order the most expense items, don't drink during an interview meal and don't talk with your mouth full—which means you may not get to eat a lot.

Don't be too familiar or informal. Never forget that it's all part of the evaluation process. I've eliminated candidates during meals when they forgot they were candidates.

After the Interview

When it's all over and you've left the building take time to reflect on what happened, how you did and what you'd like to be able to do over. Take notes on who you met and what you learned about them. Develop a plan for following up and anything you need to work on if you're invited back. Write down questions you need to practice answering. Use the interview as a learning experience to get better until you nail it and get an offer.

TOUGH QUESTIONS

Everyone has questions they hate to be asked. And interviewers love to find tough questions! Tough questions and tough interviews can help you really shine if you're prepared.

Many years ago I had the responsibility of building a new department. I read books on interviewing and came across a great suggestion. I wrote down twenty interview questions and when the candidates came in I handed them the list and asked them to answer each question in order without any responses or feedback from me. It was a fascinating process. Most of the candidates rambled, stumbled or broke down. Out of fifteen candidates, only two went down the list and answered the questions with short, concise answers. Both were invited back and I eventually offered both of them a position. What should have been an easy interview became difficult because most of the candidates were unprepared.

Be prepared. Be ready for tough questions and unusual interview techniques. If you're ready and see these situations as an opportunity you'll do great.

Questions are usually tough for two reasons. One, you aren't ready to answer them. Or two, you don't want to talk about the subject matter. To be successful you have to prepare and practice giving answers that are both truthful and positive.

Here are some of the basic categories of questions and suggestions on how to deal with them.

Tell Me About a Time . . .
When you had to deal with a co-worker who _____
When you took the time to share the credit with _____
When you didn't work well with a _____
When you worked with someone you didn't like
When you misjudged a person
When you were faced with conflicting priorities

"Tell me about" questions are softballs, even if the question isn't one you have an answer for. You're being given the chance to talk about your skills and abilities and demonstrate how you dealt with challenges someplace else.

There are two elements to a good answer for a "Tell me about" question. The first is the story that responds to the question. The second is the solution that showcases your skills and supports your message.

If you're asked to tell about a conflict you resolved, tell a story about a conflict that doesn't cast anyone in a bad light—

"In my last position I had a significant disagreement with a fellow worker on how to solve a client's problem."

This is the conflict the question asked for. You don't want to call the other employee an idiot. You want to demonstrate your ability to solve the problem and to get along with someone who doesn't agree with you. So here's the story that showcases your skills and experience:

"After a long discussion with the other employee, I realized that he had some good points and I modified my plan. But it was my client and it was my responsibility to solve the problem. I made a decision that worked and the client was very happy."

Always be grateful for "Tell me about" questions. Think of a simple story and tell it with enthusiasm and emphasize your strengths and your message.

How Do You or Would You . . .
How do you get along with older (younger) co-workers?
How do you balance life and work?
How do you stay organized?
How would you deal with an angry client?
How do you communicate—calling, email, text?

"How do you" questions are usually specific to the job requirements and most of them can be anticipated from the job description. But some of them are general in scope and have to do with basic skills and issues, like the example questions above.

Answer "How do you" questions with short stories that illustrate what you have done. It's not enough to say that you get along with younger workers. That's not a memorable answer and there's little credibility in it.

Give details. Talk about a co-worker who helped you learn something, with whom you socialized or you mentored. Don't worry about getting too specific; use humor if you can.

"In my current department we have young employees and one of our challenges was to get the groups to work together as a team. Last summer I organized a golf league and worked hard to get everyone involved. In the winter we had a couple of video game events. I learned I'm a much better golfer than video gamer!"

If you're the younger employee, the question would be about how you work with or manage older employees. The best answers include enthusiasm, confidence and respect. It's great to be a young prodigy—but one liners and arrogance are for TV scripts, not job interviews.

Failure . . .
Describe a decision you made that was a failure
Tell me about a time when you failed
What was your biggest failure or mistake?
Tell me about a time you took a stand and you were wrong
What is your biggest weakness?

Interviewers are obsessed with failure. They don't want you to ever fail if they hire you, but they know you've failed in the past and they know it's an uncomfortable topic for everyone. You have to be able to talk about failures and weaknesses; so come up with examples and practice talking about them. Show how failure helped you to grow, or how you're identified a weakness and you're in the process of overcoming it.

Have a story about a professional mistake that didn't cost your employer money or hurt anyone. When I was a new manager I hired someone who was all wrong for a position. I talk about this experience, what I learned and how I rectified the problem. I worked with the new employee and when it became clear she was wasn't going to work out, I helped her find another position in the company that suited her strengths and skills. I candidly admit that I've made other mistakes that weren't as easy to fix.

But this is my answer to this interview question because I get to pick the story to tell.

When asked about weaknesses, talk about technical skills you're working on improving. I supervised a woman who wasn't good at writing letters. I encouraged her to take some college classes in business and technical writing. When she was interviewing for a new position she was able to talk about a weakness that she had worked hard to improve.

Don't try and con the interviewers with an answer that your weakness is that you work too hard or you're too hard on yourself. You have to have an answer prepared for these types of questions. You want to be able to answer the question seriously and directly, while staying on message and demonstrating that even though you're human, you're a great human to have as an employee!

Why . . .
Why do you think you will be successful at this job?
Why do you want to leave your current position?
Why have you been unemployed for six months?
Why did you leave each of your previous positions?

"Why" questions are catch-all questions, and many "why" questions fall into other categories. But sometimes you'll be asked a question about your motivations for what you're doing. Like, why are you here being grilled by strangers for an opportunity that doesn't look any better than what you have now?

So why are you looking? Why have you done what you've done and why aren't you doing what you want to do? You need to know these answers before you can intelligently answer probing "why" questions.

As a hiring manager I tried to identify the people who wanted a new job so they could leave behind the problems they created in an old job. I was concerned about job hoppers and "green grass" people—hoping the grass was greener on our side of the fence. As a job applicant you have to be able to convince decision-makers that you have a good reason for wanting to join them, that you have a strategy for your career and that this opportunity is part of that strategy.

Who are You . . .
Are you a risk taker?
If you could, what would you do differently in your career?
Who has influenced you the most?
How do you measure success?
Do you consider yourself successful?
Describe your dream job

"Who are you" questions are different from the "why" questions in that the interviewer isn't looking for problems; he or she really wants to know what makes you tick, who you are and whether you'll be a good fit in the position.

There is one really important thing to remember when answering "who are you" questions . . . the interview is not really about you. The interview is about how well you meet their needs. It's about how well you'll fit in and whether you'll add value to the organization. So as tempting as it will be to answer these questions with soul exposing answers—don't.

Stay on message. Your message is that you will make the organization more successful if they hire you. Don't talk about your life's search for Jedi powers unless it's applicable to the position. Stay professional and use "who are you" questions to emphasize your strengths and desire to contribute and grow in a meaningful way with this organization.

Hypothetical or Alternate Universe . . .
If you could have lunch with anyone (alive or deceased), who would it be?
If you were the CEO of this company what would be the top two things that you would do?
If you could be a celebrity, what kind of celebrity would you be?
If your lawn was blue would you still have to mow it once a week?

"Hypothetical" questions always includes a component that isn't or couldn't be true. For example, any question that starts out "if money wasn't an issue" is a hypothetical question; because money is always an issue. The problem you have as an interviewee is that you have to come up with serious answers.

I was once asked what I would have done different if I had been a founding partner of a company—twenty years before I was born! The answer that came to me was that I wouldn't have hired a decision-maker who asked such a stupid question, but that wasn't going to help me make the sale. I answered that I hoped that in fifty years people were as impressed with my contribution to the company, and that I would have a positive impact and leave a great legacy. I later learned that the interviewers thought this was one of the best answers they had to this question; they never noticed that I didn't come close to actually answering the question.

The more absurd the hypothetical component of the question is, the more license you have to ignore it. Try to figure out what characteristic the interviewer is trying to find or discuss. You have to answer the question. But you don't have to buy into absurd conditions. Use hypothetical questions to be creative. Have fun with your answers and demonstrate your ability to deal with ambiguity.

Stupid Questions . . .
If you were an animal what would you be?
If you could be any animal on a carousel, what would it be?
What's your favorite game/movie/song?
Convince me to hire you

Someone once said there are no stupid questions in a job interview, only stupid answers. That's nonsense! Most interviewers are not professional interviewers. Managers use guidelines or a book on interviewing. Which means not all interviewers are good at it and all of them ask stupid questions sometimes.

If the question is stupid, don't say so. Just give a short answer with a smile and move on. If you can tie your answer to your message go for it. But it's hard to tie what kind of an animal I'd be to my leadership skills . . .

Google Questions . . .
How many intelligent civilizations are there in our Galaxy?
You have a closet full of shirts and it's hard to find a shirt, how do you organize your shirts to make it easier?
There's a latency problem in your department. Diagnose it.
How many piano tuners are there in California?

Google has turned interviewing into an art form; an annoying and abstract art form. Their interview questions have a reputation for being absurd and challenging. And other companies have started to follow their example.

Many Google interview questions ask for knowledge you don't have or answers that can't be confirmed. The interviewer isn't really concerned about the final answer at all. They want to hear how you come up with an answer. How do you approach the problem?

If you're asked how many piano tuners there are in California, your interviewer doesn't have a clue what the right answer is. You could look at him and say the answer is 3,236, but that's the wrong interview answer. The right interview answer is a story with assumptions and simple math about how many people in California own pianos, how often they need to be tuned and how many tuners, working five days a week who are able to tune three pianos a day it would take. The interviewer wants to hear about how you approach solving the problem and well you think through the issues.

Don't worry about getting the right answer to this type of question. Be creative in coming up with a solution. Use humor and engage the interviewer . . . and you'll do fine.

Issues

Do you remember all those potential employment issues you glossed over in your resume? It's harder to do that in an interview. When you're asked tough questions, you have to answer them. Lying during the hiring process is grounds for termination when the truth comes out. Some issues become evident as soon as you walk into an interview. Age, weight, disabilities, race and appearance are obvious the moment you arrive. Discrimination may be illegal, but these factors still play a role in the interview process. Right or wrong, legal or illegal, these may be issues that you have to deal with.

Other problems are more subtle, like poor job performance, past terminations, a criminal history that comes up in a background check, or health problems. Questions may be asked about excessive job hopping, multiple breaks in employment or other red flags in your employment history. Worse, these issues can come up because of information you've made available through social websites. You have to be prepared to answer questions about these issues and resolve an employer's concerns.

If questions are asked about past performance or behavioral problems, explain what you've done to change. Don't blame circumstances or past employers. Don't talk about the idiots you worked for before. Stress the value you add and be willing to make commitments that you'll keep.

For issues you have less control over—physical appearance, disability or race—you may simply have to work harder to find a job. This isn't about what's right or fair. It's about taking control of your life.

If you have additional obstacles, you can complain and give up—or you can get stronger and overcome the obstacles. Be better-educated, more skilled and more positive. Have a perfect resume and become a skilled interviewee. Make it hard for an employer to not want the incredible value you'll bring to the position. When you don't get an offer, move on to the next potential employer.

INTERVIEW MISTAKES

The internet is full of stories about people who show up on the wrong day, don't show up at all or when they do there's some glaring mistake that ruins the interview—and their chance at getting the job. Most mistakes can be avoided by being prepared and showing up with a desire to get the job.

Here are some mistakes that are much too common. Avoid them.

Don't Tell Jokes

I understand the desire to break the ice. Laughing together is a good thing in an interview. But I've have numerous candidates try to tell jokes, not personal stories, that either weren't funny or were potentially offensive. A joke won't help your message. It's not about you and it's not about what you can do for me. Avoid any story that attempts to be funny at someone else's expense. I don't want to the object of one of your stories in the future so I probably won't hire you.

Be careful not to perform a comedy routine in the interview. An occasional one-liner is okay, but using every answer to solicit laughter distracts the interviewers. Unless the job is for some kind of performance role, don't turn the interview into a laugh track.

Don't Dress Inappropriately

By inappropriately I mean anything that distracts from our conversation or embarrasses me or should embarrass you. Don't dress like you're on a reality TV show.

I've had men show up with clothes that were too tight, too casual or too extreme; women who arrived in clothes that exposed themselves or left too little to the imagination. I know I'm conservative, but in working with hundreds of companies and talking to hiring managers from across many fields, very few appreciate over-sexualized dress for an interview. And when clothes catch a decision-maker's attention it's usually for the wrong reasons.

Look like a professional. Be you, but don't mistake an interview for a night on the town. Look good, make an impression and then don't let your clothes be an issue.

Don't Chew

Anything! Don't chew gum, don't chew on your hair, don't chew your pen or pencil, don't chew your nails, don't play with your lips or your teeth—use your mouth for talking.

No BO

On several occasions I've had to move an interview from a small room to the biggest room I could find because of body odor. It was usually caused by excessive perfume or cologne, but I've also had candidates who could have showered better.

Be aware of how you smell . . . please. The sense of smell is a powerful tool for triggering memory—the last thing you want is to create a bad memory that will last forever. If you think there's the possibility of an issue ask someone you trust to tell you the truth. Don't eliminate yourself as a viable candidate because of something you can control.

Electronics

Turn off cell phones, computers and any other electronic device you bring with you to an interview. I've had candidates who texted during interviews and I've known of candidates who took phone calls. If you can't turn off your electronic toys during an interview for a job you need or want, you have a serious problem.

I've mentioned this in other chapters, but leave your phone off until you're out of the building. Don't make or take calls if you're being driven by someone from the company. As long as you're with a company employee or in the building you're still interviewing and what you say and how you act can get back to the decision-makers.

There are so many things you don't have control over that it's crucial that you control the things you do. Be alert, stay focused and be professional.

Following Up

You've left the interview. You're hoping for a follow-up interview, or even an offer. What do you do now? There are a couple of things you can do to maintain contact and stay in consideration.

Get Contact Information

Always ask for phone numbers and email addresses from the people you meet in interviews—for their business cards. You want information that allows you contact decision-makers directly.

Follow Up on Answers

A technique that I've used successfully is to identify a question, issue or discussion during the interview that I can use as an excuse to contact a decision-maker. If you mention an article or a book that you've read, ask if you can send the interviewer a copy of the article or the name of the book. Or, if you don't know the answer to a question during the interview, ask for permission to follow up later and then do it. This gives you a reason to send the information with a personal note. It's a great way to maintain contact or even develop a correspondence.

Clarify a Response

I don't do this very often but occasionally I realize that I messed up a response to a question; for example I suddenly realize that I completely misunderstood the question. In these rare cases I'll send an email or letter explaining my concern that I misunderstood the question and give the response I should have given. The two or three times I've done this I included an explanation that I would do the same thing when dealing with clients or customers, because I want to be sure that there are no misunderstandings.

I only do this when I'm sure I've blown a significant answer in the interview. This form of confession gives me another chance and I have little to lose since I didn't give a great answer in the first place. On the other hand, I can't tell you that this has worked either.

Thank You Notes

I like to send a short note or letter following up and thanking interviewers for their time. I try to make it personal and relate back to specific discussions or things I learned in the process. I know from experience that very few applicants follow-up with personal notes or professional correspondence. Done right it can help you set yourself apart from other candidates.

Be Patient

Don't keep calling to ask if a decision's been made or begging for information. It's too easy for your persistence to become their irritation. When you leave the interview you should have an idea of their time-frame for the hiring process. But, their best intentions can drag on for long periods of time. The bigger the company the longer it takes to get all of the decision-makers and staff together to make decisions. It's frustrating, especially when you're unemployed. Be patient.

Sometimes I'll follow-up after several weeks and ask for an update. If they answer that the process is ongoing I'll usually ask for permission to contact them again in a couple of weeks. I try to find someone in the process who will be the least irritated by my inquiries, usually an HR representative.

The only time I apply pressure is if I get an offer from another company and I want to see if there's a chance of a better offer. I try to go straight to the decision-makers and let them know that I need to make a decision.

Keep Looking

It's important not to stop your search while waiting to hear from a company. It can be discouraging to put your job hunt on hold and then get a rejection. To be successful you need to keep looking, applying and interviewing. Don't stop looking until you accept an offer.

Perfect Resumes & Successful Interviews

This is the last chapter. It's my attempt to motivate you to keep going until you succeed. I hope you've found valuable ideas and guidance as you look for a job or a better opportunity. It can be hard, it takes time . . . but don't give up.

Job hunting is a difficult process. It requires you to intentionally expose yourself to the kinds of activities that most of us try to avoid: sales, public speaking, writing, test taking and interrogations. But mastering the skills needed for a successful job hunt can serve you throughout your career.

Being able to create and articulate a marketing message is something you should do even when you have a job. It helps you tell clients, peers, managers and potential managers who you are.

Defining your skills, evaluating your accomplishments, working on your resume, and developing your self-promotion skills are things you should do even if you're not looking for a new job. As I learned through the years, everything can change on any given day. You never know when opportunities will suddenly appear—if you're ready for them. Or when challenges will develop that will be easier to overcome if you have a network, skills and a strategy.

You can do it. Getting a job is about making a sale. One sale. And you're the best person to get the job done. Become an expert on how you can make a difference. Keep improving your product. Control what you can control. Don't stress over what you can't control.

Remember that finding a job is a numbers game. Don't take rejection personally because it's not personal. Accept that someone made a decision. You don't have to like it. But you do have to keep going.

Have faith in yourself. You're a person who can and will succeed. You only fail if you give up. So don't give up.

APPENDIX 1
YOUR TARGET—YOUR DREAM JOB

Here's a list of questions you can answer to define your dream job—not that you're guaranteed to get it, but if you don't define it it's unlikely to fall in your lap. Most important, having high expectations will help you stay motivated to keep looking. Job hunting is hard enough, but it's even harder if you're not excited about the job you think you're going to find.

- ✓ What is your job title?
- ✓ What are your responsibilities?
- ✓ Describe where you work:
- ✓ Describe your boss:
- ✓ Describe your typical day:
- ✓ Where do you work?
- ✓ Who are your customers?
- ✓ What problems do you solve?
- ✓ When do you start every day?
- ✓ When do you finish the day?
- ✓ How much do you travel?
- ✓ Describe your benefits:
- ✓ How are you creative in this position?
- ✓ Why are you appreciated?
- ✓ What is your future here?
- ✓ What is the product you make or the service you provide?
- ✓ Describe your office or work space:
- ✓ Describe your coworkers:
- ✓ What are the company's values?
- ✓ How are you compensated—how much and why?
- ✓ How are your rewarded for exceptional performance?
- ✓ What does exceptional performance look like?
- ✓ What are the required skills?

- ✓ How is success measured in this company and for this position?
- ✓ What are your accountabilities?
- ✓ What are you learning from this job?
- ✓ What's the worst thing about this job?
- ✓ What's the best thing about this job:

Use these answers to write a job description for this position. Make it as detailed as possible. List the requirements, the duties and responsibilities. This is your target. You'll create a general resume for this job.

HELP WANTED—MY JOB

APPENDIX 2
YOUR PERSONAL INVENTORY

List each experience along with the corresponding accomplishments and the skills you developed through each one.

Here's an example of the general kind of information you should include in your personal inventory:

EXPERIENCE	ACCOMPLISHMENTS	SKILLS
Education—High school, college, graduate studies, licenses, certifications, continuing education, professional continuing education. Include dates and locations of institutions.	Grades Majors and minors Extra-curricular activities Classes you excelled in Recognition Part-time jobs	COMMUNICATION Speaking, Presentations Conversation Listening Training, Teaching Participation, Networking Interviewing Letters, Proposals, Reports, Manuals, Press Releases, Articles WORK SKILLS
Employment—Position, title, supervisor, pay and time period. List each position separately.	Official Responsibilities Special Projects Accountabilities Management Experience Authority Levels Sales Responsibility Account Handling Problem Resolution Customer Service Budget / Planning Special Events Speaking or Training Technology Experience (including specific industry application	Assessment/Analytical Skills Negotiation Marketing and Sales Workflow Improvement Productivity and Efficiency Problem-solving Conflict Resolution Finishing Time Management Customer Service and Satisfaction Client Support MANAGEMENT Goals and Policies Setting Standards Establishing Controls

	experience) Employee Development Licenses or Certificates Problems with Position Reason for Termination	Training Personnel Development Motivation Decision Making Operations and Operating Procedures Developing Structural Organization Planning
Volunteer Work—Organizations, locations, title, time invested. This can include community, athletic, religious or volunteer positions where you have meaningfully participated.	Special events or projects Positions held Regular Responsibilities Regular Participation Conferences Training	Organizing Recruiting, Hiring, and Terminating Performance Evaluation Discipline Team Building PLANNING Setting Objectives and Goals Establishing Priorities
Professional Organizations—Licensing or professional organizations you have participated in.	Licenses Continuing Education Training Professional Designations Conferences Contributions Special Events or Projects	Forecasting Scheduling Resource Requirements INNOVATION Product Development Promotional Ideas Strategies Designs TECHNICAL KNOWLEDGE
Hobbies or Projects—Special activities you have dedicated substantial time or resources to.	Training Affiliations Organizations Accomplishments Designations	Government Relations Technical Skills & Experience People & Experts Education and Training IT SKILLS Word Processing Spreadsheets/ Modeling Graphic Presentation Database Management Specific Applications

Start your own personal inventory by listing your experiences, accomplishments and skills using the chart above. Hopefully you'll need more room than this, but go ahead and get started.

Some thoughts to keep in mind:

Don't downplay your abilities, if you believe you have a skill or can take credit for an accomplishment, include it.

Think back as far as you can and include every experience and accomplishment. You may want to get some help from others who have known you for a while.

Repeat accomplishments and skills if they have been part of multiple experiences. This will help you identify patterns and strengths.

Include negative experiences, especially if they keep reoccurring, because that can help you identify areas where you can improve and problems you'll need to explain.

EXPERIENCE	ACCOMPLISHMENTS	SKILLS

Review your skills and accomplishments. Do you see any patterns? Hopefully you're already aware of your major accomplishments and the skills that made them possible, but you may find a few surprises.

Make two more lists: accomplishments and skills. From your inventory identify your most significant accomplishments and your best skills. Your list of accomplishments will be the experiences you want to share with employers. The skills are what you are selling as a professional.

ACCOMPLISHMENTS	SKILLS
1.	1.
2.	2.
3.	3.
4.	4.
5.	5.
6.	6.
7.	7.
8.	8.
9.	9.
10.	10.

Now go back to the lists of accomplishments and skills you just created. Circle your top three accomplishments and your five most significant and developed skills. If you had ten minutes to give a presentation about yourself to a group of decision-makers, which experiences would you talk about? When did you really contribute, make a difference or overcome odds? Which skills would you focus on as being the essence of who you are and what you can do?

Now, use these three accomplishments and five skills to write a paragraph that describes you—the product an employer should buy.

You

APPENDIX 3
PRACTICE INTERVIEW QUESTIONS

1. What do you find most frustrating about work?
2. Tell me about a project that got you really excited.
3. How do you define a job well done?
4. Under what conditions do you work best?
5. What is the greatest strength you would bring to this position?
6. What is your biggest weakness or deficiency?
7. What did you enjoy most about your last job?
8. Where do you see yourself in five years?
9. What does success means to you?
10. What does failure mean to you?
11. Were you successful in your last job?
12. Do you set goals for yourself? How?
13. Tell me about a work situation that required excellent communication skills.
14. Do you prefer to speak directly with someone or send a memo?
15. How would you grade your ability to communicate with upper-level management, customers, and peers?
16. What were the biggest challenges in your job?
17. How did you handle those challenges?
18. Tell me about the last time you took a risk. What was it? Was it the right decision?
19. How important is communication and interaction with others on your job?
20. Tell me about your last work emergency.
21. Give an example of a time you went above and beyond to get a job done.
22. What makes you impatient at work?
23. Tell me about deadlines you had in a job.
24. Do you like working in a fast-paced environment?
25. What decisions are most difficult for you?
26. What is the most difficult work situation you have ever had?
27. What do you do when you're having trouble with your job?
28. What do you feel an employer owes an employee?

29. If your boss tells you to do something you know is wrong, what would you do?
30. What are things you and your boss disagree about?
31. Have you ever had your work or an idea criticized? How did you handle it?
32. Tell me about the best manager you ever had. What about the worst? What made them the best or the worst?
33. What is the biggest failure you've had in your career? Why do you believe it was your biggest failure?
34. What was the most important project you've worked on?
35. What was the outcome of that project?
36. How have you added value to your employers?
37. What have you done to increase your output in a position?
38. What types of people have trouble getting along with you?
39. Do you prefer to work by yourself or with others?
40. Tell me about a time you had a conflict with a co-worker and how you resolved it.
41. How would your coworkers describe you?
42. What kind of people did you have contact with on your previous jobs (titles/positions)?
43. Define cooperation.
44. Tell me about an occasion when you pulled a team together.
45. What do you find most challenging in working with coworkers?
46. Do you function more effectively as a team member or as an individual contributor?
47. Describe the most difficult customer experience you have had. How did you handle it?
48. When you know you are right and others disagree with you, how do you handle it?
49. How do you build consensus?
50. What interests you about this job?
51. Why do you want this job?
52. Why do you think you have the right attributes or experience for this position?
53. Are you overqualified for this job?
54. What can you do for this company?
55. Why should we hire you?

56 If you were at a business lunch and you ordered a rare steak and they brought it to you well done, what would you do?
57 If I were to let you write your job description for the next year, what would it say?
58 If you could be anywhere in the world right now, where would you be?
59 How would you feel about working for someone who knows less than you do?
60 Was there a person in your career who really made a difference?
61 What's the last book you read?
62 If you were me, what questions would you ask you?
63 Do you have any questions for me?
64 What are three positive things your last boss would say about you?
65 What negative thing would your last boss say about you?
66 What do you know about our company?
67 How long will it take for you to make a significant contribution?
68 Have you ever been on a team where someone was not pulling their weight? How did you handle it?
69 What three character traits would your friends use to describe you?
70 If you were interviewing someone for this position, what traits would you look for?
71 What do you do in your spare time?
72 Tell me one thing about yourself you wouldn't want me to know.
73 Tell me the difference between *good* and *exceptional.*
74 What are three positive character traits you don't have?
75 What's the best movie you've seen (or book you've read) in the last year?
76 How do you stay organized?

Printed in Germany
by Amazon Distribution
GmbH, Leipzig